Praise for
For Men Only

"Once again, Shaunti and Jeff Feldhahn have unearthed a treasure chest of insights that are not only eyeopening but life-changing."

—ANDY STANLEY, senior pastor of North Point,
Alpharetta, Georgia; best-selling author

"In our weekly couples' study, we read and discussed both *For Women Only* and *For Men Only* over the course of several months. They were fascinating and very helpful. The findings in *For Men Only* about how women think are so enlightening. My wife and I think these books should be required premarital reading!"

—Comedian JEFF FOXWORTHY

"When we featured Shaunti's books on *FamilyLife Today,* the phone rang off the hook! When Shaunti and Jeff come back on our broadcast, I'm buying some more phones. *For Men Only* is fresh and relevant—good stuff for every marriage. Read it!"

—DENNIS RAINEY, president of FamilyLife Today

"Most of my work helping passive Christian men become more like Jesus involves how best to relate to women. I'm going to make sure to keep a case of the Feldhahns' excellent book handy at all times."

—PAUL COUGHLIN, author of *No More Christian Nice Guy*

"If you've ever asked, 'Why does she do, think, or say that?' then you've got to read this book. Shaunti and Jeff not only answer this question, they eliminate the confusion that has kept far too many men from bridging the gender gap."

—DRS. LES AND LESLIE PARROTT, best-selling authors of *Love Talk*

"Men, we're supposed to love our wives and live with them in an understanding way. That's the clear assignment God gives each of us in the Scriptures. So buy this book, read it a couple of times, underline a few key ideas, and then keep it where you can review it regularly. It will help you be the husband God wants you to be."

—BOB LEPINE, cohost of *FamilyLife Today*

Praise for
For Men Only and *For Women Only*

"Whenever Shaunti Feldhahn appears as a guest on the *Focus on the Family* radio program, we know that listener response will be enthusiastic. She has a way of connecting with the audience that is unique and compelling. We're thankful for the unique perspective she provides not only to the Christian community but to the culture at large."

—JIM DALY, president of Focus on the Family

"These are the books I pass out to people as the best on the subject. Shaunti Feldhahn has the rare ability to do impeccable research and then make her findings incredibly practical. There is something to learn on every page."

—JIM BURNS, PhD, president of HomeWord; author
of *Creating an Intimate Marriage*

"Whatever Shaunti Feldhahn researches, read. Actually, do more than read...study! Shaunti's ability to ask the right questions, find the right answers, and communicate the results clearly and practically sets her apart as a gifted researcher. Her content guides and changes lives."

—EMERSON EGGERICHS, PhD, best-selling author
of *Love and Respect*

"Shaunti Feldhahn has a unique gift for helping men understand women, and women, men. Her books, *For Women Only* and *For Men Only,* are the best I know at providing rich and practical gender understanding that can be used immediately. I highly recommend both all the time!"

—ROBERT LEWIS, author of *Raising a Modern-Day Knight;*
founder of Men's Fraternity

for
men
only

Other Books by Shaunti and Jeff Feldhahn

For Women Only
by Shaunti Feldhahn

For Young Men Only
by Jeff Feldhahn and Eric Rice
with Shaunti Feldhahn

For Young Women Only
by Shaunti Feldhahn and Lisa Rice

For Parents Only
by Shaunti Feldhahn and Lisa Rice

Made to Crave for Young Women
by Lysa TerKeurst and Shaunti Feldhahn

For Women Only in the Workplace
by Shaunti Feldhahn

The Male Factor
by Shaunti Feldhahn

The Life Ready Woman
by Shaunti Feldhahn and Robert Lewis

Shaunti and Jeff Feldhahn

for

A Straightforward Guide to the Inner Lives of Women

men

REVISED AND UPDATED EDITION

only

MULTNOMAH
BOOKS

For Men Only

Scripture quotations and paraphrases are taken from the following versions: The Holy Bible, New International Version®, NIV®. Copyright © 1973, 1978, 1984 by Biblica Inc.™ Used by permission of Zondervan. All rights reserved worldwide. www.zondervan.com. The Holy Bible, English Standard Version, copyright © 2001 by Crossway Bibles, a division of Good News Publishers. Used by permission. All rights reserved.

Details in some anecdotes and stories have been changed to protect the identities of the persons involved.

Hardcover ISBN 978-1-60142-445-7
eBook ISBN 978-1-60142-209-5

Copyright © 2006, 2013 by Veritas Enterprises Inc.

Cover design by Mark D. Ford

Published in association with the literary agency of Calvin W. Edwards, 1220 Austin Glen Drive, Atlanta, GA 30338.

Published in the United States by Multnomah, an imprint of the Crown Publishing Group, a division of Penguin Random House LLC, New York.

MULTNOMAH® and its mountain colophon are registered trademarks of Penguin Random House LLC.

Library of Congress Cataloging-in-Publication Data
Feldhahn, Shaunti Christine.
    For men only : a straightforward guide to the inner lives of women / Shaunti and Jeff Feldhahn. — Revised Edition.
      pages cm
    Includes bibliographical references.
    ISBN 978-1-60142-445-7 — ISBN 978-1-60142-209-5 (electronic)
  1. Men (Christian theology) 2. Christian men—Conduct of life. I. Feldhahn, Jeff. II. Title.
    BT703.5.F45 2013
    248.8'42—dc23

                                                    2012044585

Printed in the United States of America
2018—Revised Edition

12

Special Sales
Most Multnomah books are available at special quantity discounts when purchased in bulk by corporations, organizations, and special-interest groups. Custom imprinting or excerpting can also be done to fit special needs. For information, please e-mail specialmarketscms @penguinrandomhouse.com or call 1-800-603-7051.

To our parents,
who taught us through their
example that working to
understand each other
is worth it.

Contents

RETHINKING RANDOM

*Why you need a new map
of the female universe*

ike some guys I know, you might be tempted to skip this introduction and jump right to the sex chapter. And if you're chuckling right now, it probably means you already did. Or were about to. It's not a bad choice, actually. Just a little self-defeating. If you've been in a committed relationship with a woman for more than, say, a day, you know that going just for what you want isn't actually going to get you what you want for very long.

A week, maybe?

But let's be honest—one of the main reasons you're looking at this book is because you are trying to get something you want. Not sex (well, not just sex), but a more fulfilling, harmonious relationship with your wife, one that isn't quite so hard or confusing. And the back cover gave you the wild idea that understanding her might actually be possible.

Either that or for some reason the woman in question just handed you this book.

Hmm.

Well, either way, take a look at the revelations we've uncovered. We think you'll be convinced. Each chapter explains things about the woman you love that may have often left you feeling helpless, confused, or just plain angry. Each chapter points out simple, doable solutions. The only genius required is that you make a decision up-front that you're willing to think differently. This is a short book, but if you read it cover to cover, you'll walk away with your eyes opened to things you may have never before understood about your wife or girlfriend.

> Each chapter points out simple, doable solutions.

That's what happened with me—Jeff. And I'm just your average, semi-confused guy. (Actually, sometimes *totally confused* is more accurate.) And since we average, semi-confused guys have to stick together, that's why, even though Shaunti and I are both authoring this book, I'll be the one doing the talking.

FIRST, SOME BACKGROUND

In 2004 Shaunti published *For Women Only: What You Need to Know About the Inner Lives of Men,* which quickly became a bestseller. Based on nationally representative surveys, focus groups, personal interviews, and other research with thousands of men, it opened women's eyes to things that most of us guys had always wished our wife or girlfriend knew. Things like, most of us need to feel *respected* even more than loved. Or that besides just getting enough sex, we also have a huge need to feel sexually *desired* by our wives.

I'm not sure exactly why, but women everywhere were shocked. And by the flood of letters from around the country—from both women *and* their grateful husbands—Shaunti and I have seen how much good can come when the opposite sex finally has their eyes opened to things they simply didn't understand before.

In this book, the shock is on the other foot. Now it's their turn to exclaim to us, "I can't believe you didn't already know that!"

When Shaunti's publisher first approached us about doing a companion book to *For Women Only* to help men understand women, I had two major concerns. First, I didn't think guys would read a "relationship" book. For most of us, the last relationship

Introduction

book we read was in premarital counseling—and then only because we were forced to. But more to the point, I doubted that
women could ever be understood. Compared to other complex
matters—like the tides, say, or how to figure a baseball pitcher's
ERA—women seemed unknowable. Random even.

> I'm not sure exactly why, but women
> everywhere were shocked by how men
> thought.

I explained my skepticism to one early focus group of women:

JEFF: Guys tend to think that women are random. We
think, *I pulled this lever last week and got a certain
reaction. But when I pulled that same lever this
week, I got a totally different reaction.* That's
random!

WOMAN IN GROUP: But we aren't random! If you pull
the lever and get a different reaction, either you're
pulling a different lever or you're pulling it in a
different way.

SHAUNTI: What men need is a sort of map to their
wives or girlfriends. Because we *can* be mapped.
We can be known and understood—firm
ground.

JEFF: Uh, no. See, guys think of a woman as a swamp. You can't see where you're stepping, and sooner or later you just know you're going to get stuck in quicksand. And the more you struggle to get free, the deeper you get sucked in. So every guy on the planet knows that the best thing to do is just shut down and not struggle and hope somebody comes along to rescue you.

When I came to, Shaunti and the other women in the focus group assured me—and I have since seen for myself—that guys don't have to live in a swamp. That realization led us to the eventual subtitle of this book: *A Straightforward Guide to the Inner Lives of Women*.

> "Guys think of a woman as a swamp. You can't see where you're stepping, and sooner or later you just know you're going to get stuck in quicksand."

We have been astounded and humbled at the reaction to these simple, eyeopening truths. In fact, the book you are holding is actually the second edition of this book—which was needed because there was clearly a desire for this ongoing research.

Both *For Women Only* and *For Men Only* sparked a huge wave of encouragement and hope among ordinary men and

Introduction

women just like me and Shaunti, selling two million copies in twenty-two languages. We were flooded with e-mails and comments from men and women at our marriage conferences, saying things like "This saved my marriage" and "After ten years together, I finally know how to make my wife happy" and even "Jeff, I owe you one, buddy."

But since we've continued to learn new things, we also wanted to keep the book current. For this new edition, we have included some fascinating new findings, including the brain science behind *why* women sometimes think as they do. Plus we've added a new chapter—"The Reason Hiding in Her 'Unreasonable' Reaction"—that decodes those unpredictable reactions that she thinks of as, uh, normal.

After seeing the impact of this research, I realize that we really did uncover life-changing insights. Surprising truths that average guys like me *need* to hear from an average guy and be encouraged that if someone like me can learn it and do it, they can too.

THE SEVEN REVELATIONS

So let's go back to that swamp—the one we think is there but doesn't really exist. The most important key to "de-swamping" the woman in your life is to realize that some of your basic assumptions about her may be either too simplistic or flat wrong. By simplistic, I mean that we tend to operate with a partial or surface understanding of our wife or girlfriend. And to make matters worse, most guys have no idea how to make their limited understanding work in actual practice.

For example, most guys have heard that women want security. Okay. But what does that mean, exactly? A regular paycheck? A big house? It's a huge shocker to talk to hundreds of women and find that while financial security is nice, it isn't nearly as important to them as feeling emotionally secure—feeling close and confident that you will be there for her no matter what. And believe it or not, ensuring emotional security turns out to be a lot easier than ensuring the financial security you are probably busting your tail to provide.

For Men Only will help you move from surface understandings to the all-important recognition of what those things mean in everyday life with your woman. Once you start testing out these findings, you'll be amazed at the difference it makes for both of you. Because—brace yourself—you will realize that you *can* understand your wife and make her happy.

Introduction

> You will realize that you *can* understand your wife and make her happy.

Sound wildly impossible? I'll go one better. You'll see that this huge shift can happen for you and the woman you love *even if it starts out as a totally one-sided effort on your part.*

The second edition of *For Men Only* is organized around seven major findings outlined on the facing page. Some of these will be surprises to you. Some won't, at least to begin with. (But that's the thing about swamps—what you see is rarely what is really there.)

HOW WE FOUND OUT: OUR METHODOLOGY

In our initial research for this book, Shaunti and I worked for a year to identify inner "map terrain" areas that are common to most women but that most guys tend not to understand. Besides conducting hundreds of in-person interviews, we gathered huge amounts of anecdotal information at dozens of women's events where Shaunti was presenting materials from *For Women Only*. I spoke with stay-at-home moms, business owners, and secretaries; and on airplanes, in focus groups, and over Shaunti's book table while she was being mobbed at women's conferences. I sifted through hundreds of e-mails and forum postings from Shaunti's forwomenonlybook.com website.

In all these venues, I was really just the "embedded male." Like the reporters who rode with the armored cavalry divisions at the opening of the Iraq War, I kept my helmet on, my head down, and my notebook handy.

After all that research, we did a scientific, nationally representative survey. As Shaunti had done for her previous book, we

Our Surface Understanding	What That Means in Practice
She needs to feel loved.	Even if your relationship is great, your mate likely has a fundamental insecurity about your love—and when that insecurity is triggered, she may respond in ways that confuse or upset you until she feels reassured.
Women are emotional.	Women deal with multiple thoughts and emotions from their past and present all the time, at the same time—and these can't be easily dismissed.
She's impossible to figure out.	There is usually a logical reason behind her baffling words or actions—and behavior that confuses or frustrates you often signals a need she is asking you to meet.
Women want security—in other words, financial security.	Your woman needs emotional security and closeness with you so much that she will endure financial insecurity to get it.
She doesn't want you to fix it; she just wants you to listen.	When she is sharing an emotional problem, her feelings and her desire to be heard are much more important than the problem itself.
She doesn't want sex much—which means she must not want me.	Physically, women tend to crave sex less often than men do—and it is usually not related to your desirability.
She wants to look attractive.	Inside your smart, secure wife lives a little girl who deeply needs to know that you find her beautiful—and that you only have eyes for her.

Introduction

worked with survey-design expert Chuck Cowan, former chief of census design for the U.S. Census Bureau, and the well-respected survey company Decision Analyst. They came together to help us design and conduct a groundbreaking survey of four hundred women from all over the country. Since then, we've done other surveys. Adding it all up, well over six thousand women provided input for this book.

> I was really just the "embedded male." I kept my helmet on, my head down, and my notebook handy.

I know you'll be fascinated by the results. While some of the findings may be challenging or difficult to accept, most men have been surprised by how helpful many of these truths are and how *simple* they are to implement for a better, easier relationship, a happy wife (or girlfriend), and more peace in their home.

THE MAP KEY

Before we tackle the findings, here are some pointers on reading the map:

- **This book holds to a biblical worldview.** Our aim is to be relevant and revealing, no matter what your worldview is, and we surveyed women regardless of cultural background or religious beliefs. But thousands of churches now require our books before a couple gets married. And because Shaunti and I view life through our Christian faith, we have seen that these findings are consistent with biblical principles. We believe that relationships are most fulfilling when both people have a common commitment to serving Jesus. Since our focus is on what we learned through research, we do not quote heavily from Scripture, but we draw from and reference it as the only dependable guidebook for relationships.

- **This is not a comprehensive marriage book.** Since there are already many great marriage books on the market, there's no need to cover topics that other experts can tackle far better than we can or that guys already have a good handle on. (We list several recommended resources at our website, formenonlybook.com.) Instead, we focus specifically on high-leverage surprises—truths that we don't tend to get, where small, simple changes can have huge impacts. Also, while our content is probably a bit more targeted toward married men, these insights will be helpful for any male-female relationship. That said, if your relationship is seriously on the rocks, this little book will probably open your eyes in some important areas, but it is not designed to cover a crisis situation. We encourage you to get the kind of counsel and support your marriage deserves.

- **This is not an equal treatment.** Just as *For Women Only* was intentionally one-sided (and if your wife read it, you may have benefited from that fact), so is this book. Yes, you have needs too, and there certainly may be relationship issues arising because *she* doesn't understand *you*. But *For Women Only* addresses many of those, and this book is not about them. This is only about the inner lives of women, and we're focusing entirely on how men relate to women, not the other way around. (That is also why the survey polled only heterosexual women.)

- **There are exceptions to every rule.** Recognize that when I say "most women" appear to think a certain way, *most* does not mean *all*. We make generalizations out of necessity to be helpful in the widest number of circumstances. Inevitably there will be exceptions. Statistically, in fact, it is likely that some male readers will think in a way similar to their wives in one area or another. Everyone is an individual, so the goal is to have your eyes open for what is most important in *your* situation.

- **Our findings may not be politically correct, but we try to be true to the evidence.** For six years, Shaunti was a newspaper columnist on women's issues, and she sometimes received e-mails from women complaining that she was doing exactly what we intend to do in this book—making generalizations about women. Add the fact that I, as a *guy*, am daring to make those generalizations, and we recognize the potential for controversy. We don't quite know how to get around that, so we decided to just report what we learned.

> We decided to just report what we learned.

THE THING TO DO NEXT

We think that in the pages ahead you're going to receive a lot of promising invitations to try some new things. Most are incredibly simple, but they may not come naturally. At least at first. Of course, if all this were already instinctive to you, then you wouldn't be troubled by randomness, confusion, or frustration... and did I mention swamps?

My encouragement to you: Give the process time as you retrain years of incorrect assumptions and counterproductive reactions. Bring a humble attitude. Be willing to practice. Believe it can be done.

Because I've learned that it can be.

After several months as an embedded male, I was watching a movie with Shaunti one night. Halfway through, I casually mentioned that I didn't like the way one of the female characters was treating another. Shaunti sat up on the couch, grinned, and said, "You're thinking like a girl!"

Now, she meant it as high praise, but in the small midwestern town where I grew up, that kind of talk could get a guy slugged. But then I realized: maybe I *had* learned a valuable thing or two about the female universe just by listening in.

Here's hoping that you do too.

2

THE DEAL IS NEVER CLOSED

Why her "I do" will always mean "Do you?"—and what to do about it

Even if your relationship is great, your mate likely has a fundamental insecurity about your love—and when that insecurity is triggered, she may respond in ways that confuse or upset you until she feels reassured.

hink of the deals you've struck in your life. Your first car. Your first real job. Your first house. You saw what you wanted, did what you had to do to get it—and you came home with a done deal.

No deal compares to winning a wife, though. You pursued

her with all the courage, creativity, and resources you could muster. Then, one day, you closed the deal. Your wedding day was the day you proved your love to the world and to her.

Divorce stats to the contrary, I'd bet that—since you're reading this book—your marriage feels like the most obviously *closed deal* in your whole life. Right?

Well, not exactly. As we'll explain in this chapter, it just feels closed for you.

No, your wife isn't still out looking for suitors. But in an unusual and powerful way that married men don't really understand, your wife doesn't feel permanently loved once the marriage papers are signed. She may have a subconscious question about your love. She may *know* you love her, but there will be times when her *feelings* will need to be convinced and reassured. Sometimes over and over again.

THE TRUTH ABOUT "I DO"

It's no surprise that a woman needs to feel loved. What is a surprise is how easy it is for her to *not* feel loved. It turns out that buried inside most women—even those in great relationships—is a latent insecurity about whether their man *really* loves them and even whether they are truly lovable. In our research, women described it as a subconscious question: *Would he choose me all over again?* This sense of vulnerability may usually be under the surface of their minds, but when it is triggered, most women start worrying about whether the relationship is okay and show signs of distress until the concern is resolved.

You can read "show signs of distress" as "drive their man nuts" if you want.

◁ Buried inside most women—even those in great relationships—is a latent insecurity about whether their man really loves them.

Fact is, you're going to see (as I did) that many of the things that perplex and even anger us about our wife or girlfriend are *signals that she is feeling insecure about our love or the relationship.* Have you ever wondered why she:

- asks, "Do you love me?" even though you've done nothing to indicate you've changed your mind about loving her? (In fact, you said "I love you" this morning on your way out the door!)

- takes your need for space or "cave" time as an indication that you're upset with her and trying to get away from her?

- wants to talk, talk, talk about your relationship—especially at the times you least want to?

Reassurance

- seems to turn critical or angry with you for no reason you can figure?
- gets crabby or emotional and seems to push you away—but then gets even more unhappy when you *stay* away?
- gets upset or wants to punish you for spending time with the guys or doing other things away from her?

If you're like me, you react to these seemingly unrelated behaviors with confusion and frustration—or worse. If it happens a lot, you may get angry back or you may withdraw and just try to endure, hoping things will someday change. Or you may become convinced that you'll never know what she wants and could never please her if you did.

> You'll see those "drive you nuts" behaviors as red warning lights signaling a breach in your wife's confidence about whether you really love her.

But our research for *For Men Only* persuaded me that all of those behaviors are related and many are easy to resolve. Once you're clued in, you'll see those "drive you nuts" behaviors as red warning lights signaling a breach in your wife's confidence about whether you really love her. In fact, the more extreme the behavior, the more serious her doubt.

I know it sounds crazy that your wife might ever wonder whether you love her, especially when things are going fine. But as it turns out, your "I do" actually *didn't* bring permanent emotional closure, forever putting her mind to rest about your feelings for her. It doesn't erase the insecurity about your love that lives under the surface in even the most happily married woman—an insecurity that, when triggered, becomes a deeply felt uncertainty: "Do you *still* love me? Are we okay?"

Now, you might be thinking, *Surely this doesn't apply to* my *wife! She* knows *I love her!*

Yes, she probably does. But we're not talking about what she *knows logically* but rather about the *feeling* that rises up when something triggers it. And it turns out that understanding and knowing how to address *this one thing* functions as a kind of "open sesame" that brings a man a lot more peace and pleasure at home.

THREE SURPRISES (WHAT "NEVER A DONE DEAL" FEELS LIKE TO HER)

As the token embedded male for our surveys and focus groups, I was in for a number of big surprises on the subject of women's relational, triggered insecurity.

My First Surprise: How Frequently These Feelings Appear

Whereas most guys coast along, rarely thinking about the health of their relationship, it is on a woman's mind whether she wants it to be or not. Seven out of every ten women said that their relationship and how their man felt about them was anywhere from occasionally to nearly always on their minds. Fewer than 20 percent said that they wondered about it only when things were difficult. (Just 12 percent never thought about it at all.)

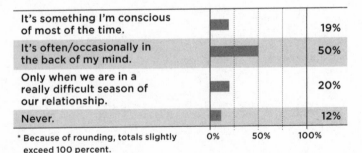

Under what circumstances do you think about your relationship, whether it is going well, or how your husband/significant other feels about you? (Choose one answer.)

It's something I'm conscious of most of the time.	19%
It's often/occasionally in the back of my mind.	50%
Only when we are in a really difficult season of our relationship.	20%
Never.	12%

* Because of rounding, totals slightly exceed 100 percent.

I'm guessing that, for most guys, "occasional" thoughts about the closeness of their relationship might boil down to birthdays, anniversaries, and when something goes drastically, obviously haywire. But when we asked women what they meant by "occasional" concern about how their man felt about them, I often heard that it meant several times a week or *whenever it was triggered* (such as by what we might consider a relatively minor spat).

We checked these results by asking the question another way and got an even stronger response. Four out of five women acknowledged sometimes feeling insecure about their man's love and the relationship. Among women under forty-five, the percentage jumped to 91 percent, and among those with children in middle school or younger, it was almost universal.

I found that we guys can understand this foreign-seeming insecurity if we compare it to one of our own. As one woman put it, "You know that record that's always running in a guy's head about providing? Well, *we* have the same fundamental concern about our relationship all the time. And if it's not going well, it can mess up everything else in our lives."

My Second Surprise: How Intensely Painful These Feelings Are

Almost every woman I asked said that she cared about her man so much that when this relational insecurity was triggered, it was very painful—sometimes almost debilitating—and it became difficult, if not impossible, for her to get it off her mind. As several women put it, "When we're at odds, nothing is right with the world until it is resolved."

Reassurance

On the survey, eight out of ten women agreed, saying that this "Does he really love me?" concern left them feeling anxious, preoccupied, emotionally withdrawn, unvalued, or depressed—and most of these were affected in visible ways. Look at the data:

When you are feeling insecure about his love or the relationship, which of the following are true <u>about your feelings</u>? (Choose all correct answers.)*

I need reassurance.	44%
I might become quite preoccupied until I get that reassurance.	20%
I withdraw emotionally.	32%
I become depressed.	28%
It affects other areas of my life.	34%
Subtotal answering one or more of above:	**74%**
It confirms my suspicion that I'm not very lovable or not worthy of his love.	10%
I feel like I'm not valued in his eyes.	26%
Nothing helps; I just need time to process alone.	9%
Total answering one or more of above:	**82%**
I never feel insecure about his love or the relationship.	18%

0%   50%   100%

* Because respondents could choose more than one answer, results do not add up to 100%

You and I have every right to think the woman we love *shouldn't* feel insecure. We're faithful, we go to work, we *do* love her...and we're still here. But just because we think our wife *should* feel secure doesn't mean that she always *does*. Which leads to my third realization.

My Third Surprise: How Resistant to Logic (That Is, My Logic) Her Feelings Remain

Shaunti points out, "It's irrelevant whether she should know logically that she's loved. If she doesn't *feel* loved, it's the same for her as if she *isn't* loved." One survey taker put it this way:

> I wish he realized that, where he processes everything based just on logic, I process information based also on emotion. He says that I know logically that he loves me, and that should be enough. But the fact is, emotionally, I don't *feel* loved.

Think about one of our own concerns that's often resistant to logic—our success at work. Even secure, competent men who are good at their jobs inwardly feel—all logic to the contrary—that they still could be just a few mistakes or industry hiccups away from everything going south, even losing their job. When things are tough at work and the economy is shaky, it makes a

Reassurance

huge difference when our boss makes a point of reassuring us that our job is secure.

In the same way, even women in good relationships feel they could be just a few bad blowups away from things going south, even losing their man's love. As one woman said, "I don't think we ever take his love for granted." So when there is any sort of trouble between you, she needs you to reassure her of your love and that the relationship is secure.

> Even women in good relationships feel they could be just a few bad blowups away from things going south.

HIDDEN TRIGGERS

In the course of everyday life in a reasonably healthy relationship, what is most likely to drive her to wonder, *Does he still love me?* Here are a few triggers:

- **Conflict.** For us, as guys, conflict is just conflict— it's not a signal or a start of something bigger. But as one woman explained, "A lot of desperate feelings surface for me when I feel like my husband is displeased with me. I know it sounds old-fashioned, and I'm a pretty independent person, but it still really affects me."

- **Withdrawal.** When we're faced with conflict, men tend to retreat into silence to escape unwanted feelings. Often we can't fully articulate something yet or we want to avoid saying something hurtful. Unfortunately, seeing her man withdraw or become moody usually generates *more* unwanted feelings for a woman. Several women described what crossed their mind this way: *What happens if he doesn't snap out of it this time?*

- **Silence.** Because women have a radar for unspoken conflict, it's pretty easy for women to jump to conclusions when their man is more withdrawn or quieter than usual. As one woman put it, "If you're quiet, it must be me." The women told me it makes a big difference when a guy sees the misunderstanding for what it is and uses it as an opportunity to reassure her. ("I'm not mad, don't worry. Just concerned about work.")

- **Her emotional bank account is depleted.** Perhaps she's exhausted, or you've been absent a lot (even necessary absences can be draining). Maybe the two of you have unresolved issues and conflicts. Regardless of the reason, even if it has nothing to do with you, her insecurity will be more easily triggered if her emotional reserves are low.

Reassurance

Once we recognize these triggers and see the red warning light for what it is—a signal that she needs to be reassured of our love—we can take some incredibly simple steps toward being part of the answer for her rather than part of the problem.

A PRACTICAL GUIDE TO TURNING OFF THE WARNING LIGHT

I hope you're seeing by now that a woman is likely to experience an undercurrent of relationship insecurity *even if* you and I are totally innocent of intent, injury, or error. (Not that we always *are*, but work with me here.) Since every day she subconsciously wonders *Does he love me?* she will be looking for clues to the answer every day.

Maybe this is what the apostle Paul had in mind when he wrote the simple admonition "Husbands, love your wives" in his letter to the church at Ephesus. I don't hear any echoes of "The deal is sealed" in his words. Or "Once you've won a wife, Bubba, you're off the hook." What I hear is much more dynamic: *Love, go on loving, continue to prove your love, keep on winning her heart with your love…*

I don't hear any echoes of "Once you've won a wife, Bubba, you're off the hook."

So how do you and I address the fact that our wives carry around this fundamental insecurity about our love? Based on our research, we see two key solutions. The first addresses her insecurity when it is triggered. The second prevents her insecurity from being triggered in the first place:

1. In the face of insecurity, reassure her.
2. Even after you've caught her, continue to pursue her.

Thankfully, both of these are completely doable for ordinary guys like you and me.

Part 1: Regular Reassurance

Once her insecurity has been triggered and her heart is anxiously wondering, *Does he really love me?* the solution is simple: reassure her that you do. Here are four ways to do that.

1. During Conflict, Reassure Her of Your Love

If you're like most guys, when you're in the middle of a conflict, you need time alone to process things. Most women we heard from react exactly the opposite—only 9 percent wanted to handle their feelings of insecurity alone.

The problem, of course, is that your pulling away to get space pushes her "Does he love me?" turmoil through the roof. If you need to get space, reassure her of your love first.

Reassurance

This is the magic bullet that almost every woman told us would make all the difference: if their man would say something like "I'm angry right now, and I need some space, but I want you to know: we're okay." On the survey, a whopping 95 percent of women said that this one step on our part would diminish or even eliminate the emotional turmoil on their part!

> The magic bullet that makes all the difference: "I'm angry right now, and I need some space, but I want you to know that we're okay."

In an emotional conflict, if your husband/significant other initiates a step to reassure you of his love, how much does it help diminish any turmoil you are feeling? (Choose one answer.)

Not at all.	5%
Some.	34%
Quite a lot.	54%
It solves it.	8%

0%   50%   100%

* Because of rounding, results slightly exceed 100 percent.

Chances are, in the midst of conflict, your woman is feeling unloved (even unlovable) and needs you to look her in the eye and tell her that you love her and you're not going anywhere.

Yes, this can be difficult. It's one thing for us to give reassurances when things are peachy, but it's quite another when we're at odds with each other and we'd rather stomp out to the garage and split a block of wood with our bare hands.

But the survey also showed that 86 percent of women said that, bolstered by our "I want you to know that we're okay" reassurance, they'd be better able to give us the space we need. (Do you see the possibilities? Reassure her of your love, *then* stomp out to the garage!) Why? Because we've reassured them on the original question: "Does he still love me?"

Suppose you and your husband/significant other are in the middle of an emotional conflict, and he eventually says, "I don't want to talk about this right now." If he were to add a reassurance, such as, "I want you to know that we're okay," would that make you more or less likely to be able to give him space? (Choose one answer.)

Much more likely.	43%
More likely.	43%
Less likely.	2%
It would have no relevance.	12%

0%   50%   100%

Reassurance

There is one final step to making this magic bullet really work. After you've had your space for a while, you have to come back and be willing to address the original issue without making her bring it up.

Easy? No. Effective? You bet. Because, as one woman said, "The fact that he comes back often matters more than the reason for the conflict in the first place."

> "The fact that he comes back often matters more than the reason for the conflict in the first place."

2. If She's Upset, Realize That She Doesn't Need Space—She Needs a Hug

When our wife or girlfriend is upset, we do what we would do with other guys: we give her space to work things out. But with few exceptions, when women are upset, they don't want space; they want a hug. I think this next comment is one of the most valuable "just do this" quotes in the book:

> All I want is him to know that half the time I'm just as confused as he is. Instead of getting upset and leaving me alone to "calm down," I just want him to come close and give me a huge hug and let me know he loves me and he wants me to feel better again.

When I shared this comment at a marriage conference, one man shouted out in a joking way (sort of), "You mean hug the porcupine?!" All the men laughed and then looked astonished when all the women shouted "Yes!" and started clapping.

Here's how one woman tried to explain it to the men: "We don't see ourselves as being that intimidating or 'prickly' when we are upset, but I guess we are. If he would just move toward me rather than away—if he would just take a deep breath and hug me instead of retreating—he'd see those porcupine quills melt."

3. If She Needs to Talk About the Relationship, Do Your Best to Listen Without Becoming Defensive

The next step is more intimidating but essential. If she *does* need to talk, try to see it as she does: a joint problem-solving session instead of an attack on *you*.

"When I tell him how I feel about something concerning our relationship, I am just trying to share my feelings so we can discuss it," one woman said. "But he takes it as criticism, and then I feel like the bad guy for bringing it up. I wish he could understand that it's important for me to be able to talk about these things and understand that I'm not just being critical."

All this research has convinced me that when most women bring up a problem, they are *not* thinking that we've failed. We need to push through our natural tendency to view what they are saying as criticism.

Reassurance

4. If She Is Being Difficult, Don't Stop—Keep Reassuring Her of Your Love

Finally, let's address a dynamic that confuses and even aggravates us: the importance of reassuring and showing love to our wife *even when* she's difficult, critical, resistant, or pushing us away. As you can probably guess, that is the ultimate sign of the "Do you really love me?" question.

It seems crazy to us, but it turns out that for many women, the more unloved she feels, the more likely she is to push her husband away or to make it hard for him to love her. She's hoping he will prove that he *really does* love her by staying put and reassuring her of his love instead. One woman provided this explanation:

> You have to realize, if a woman says, "I need to hear that you love me," and the guy dutifully says, "I love you," well, that's essentially meaningless: like she made him say something he didn't feel. So if she's feeling confused and neglected and really does want to be assured of his feelings, she can't just ask.
>
> And if they are at odds, she's maybe a little mad at him, so when he approaches her, she pushes him away *even though closeness is what she most wants!* But if he'll put aside his pride and try again, if he'll risk grabbing her hand and saying something like, "Don't go away. I

want to know what's wrong," that will break through her defenses. It tells her that no matter how she's feeling right then—*whew*—he really loves her.

Notice that this type of reassurance doesn't mean "nobly enduring her mood(s) in silence" but rather doing the intensely difficult but courageous work of not just *hugging* the porcupine but *pursuing* the porcupine. Fair warning: this will include times when we've sensed insecurity and are trying to reassure her and still get pushed away. Few things drive a guy more crazy than the sense of being tested or manipulated, and most of us soon give up in disgust. I can't tell you how many times when facing resistance, I've thought, *Fine, suit yourself. I've got to cut the lawn anyway.* And then I pretty much put the incident out of my mind.

> This type of reassurance doesn't mean "nobly enduring her mood(s) in silence."

Unfortunately a woman can't. She's still seeking the answer to the original question: "Do you still love me?" If the contentious, aggravating, push-you-away behavior is recurring, it is *because your wife truly is feeling that you don't love her—and has probably been feeling that way for some time.*

You may be trying your utmost to be a loving husband, but

clearly something is not getting through. She may need to feel loved in an entirely different way than you ever realized. So as you learn what that looks like, even if you're speechless with frustration, you're still in the game. Forget giving speeches and simply reach for her. We'll explain more in chapter 4.

Part 2: Persistent Pursuit

Now to an even more valuable tool for a man who wants to show his wife that he'd choose her all over again *today:* pursuit. Where reassurance *heals* insecurity, pursuit *prevents* a lot of insecurity. Pursuit actively makes her feel loved. In other words, it is likely to be the thing that makes you a great husband in her eyes.

> Pursuit is likely to make you a great husband in her eyes.

Pursuit is action. It's what you did when you first wanted to make her yours. It fills up her emotional bank account. And pursuit is what she still deeply needs in her marriage, even if we "close the deal" kind of guys are already on to the next big deal—completing our education, launching a career, raising kids, perfecting our golf swing...

All worthy goals, mind you. But they tend to make us forget that the pursuit of her that we thought was completed, really isn't.

One woman we interviewed recounted a common story line that captures the dilemma perfectly:

I know a woman who was divorced for quite a few years, but then this new guy started pursuing her. At first she was cautious—she was fine on her own and didn't think he was her type. But he just *wooed* her—there's no other way of putting it. He was very attentive and made it clear that he thought she was something special and that he wouldn't be dissuaded easily. He sent her flowers all the time, which is one of her "things," and dropped her little notes, and it just made her feel so special.

As he pursued her steadily like that for several years, she saw all his terrific qualities and fell hard in love. They got married—and almost immediately she began to think that something was wrong. All those little things that said "I love you" to her, well, he stopped doing them! No more flowers or notes or pursuing. It seemed to her like, once they got married, he suddenly stopped caring about her.

And now he doesn't understand why she's upset. He just says, "Of *course* I love you, honey!" and then goes on about his day. Meantime, he doesn't realize that his wife is getting seriously, seriously depressed.

Reassurance

Of course, you and I can identify with this story from the guy's side. It's common for men to think that pursuing goes with dating, not with marriage. But remember: for women, there is never a magic moment of closure when they feel permanently, fully, deeply loved. *They think that's what the rest of married life is for!* In fact, several women compared the need to feel pursued by their husbands with the need that a man has to feel sexually desired by his wife! If it's that important, what is a smart married man to do?

Big-screen answer: Give chase.

Pixil answer: Ask yourself, *What did I do when we were dating that made me so pickin' irresistible?*

> Ask yourself, *What did I do when we were dating that made me so pickin' irresistible?*

Probably you spent hours just hanging out together. You listened. You flirted. You sent e-mails or texts during the day just to say hi. You shared dreams. You said things like "I can't imagine life without you" and "I'm so glad God brought us together."

In other words, you proved to her that you were smitten.

Want a portrait of pursuit in marriage? You and I should consider that we might already be masters of it. Now that we know the chase isn't over, we just need to remember to do what came so naturally before.

Before you groan and say, "But that was exhausting. I got married so I could *stop* doing that stuff!" let me put in a reassurance of my own. I'm not talking about the big-deal events you planned to impress your bride-to-be, like the picnics in the park or the months you spent secretly getting tickets to her dream concert. I'm talking about the *little* things that speak love to her. Every. Single. Day. Like putting your arm around her in church. Or the text message that says, "I was just thinking about what a great mom you are." Or reaching to take her hand when you're walking across a parking lot.

No matter what you do, those little things say one thing: I *would* choose you all over again. Today. That reassurance—every day—goes so deep into her heart that all those buried doubts are laid to rest.

"YOU DIDN'T COME AFTER ME"

Maybe you remember the 1998 remake of the old Disney movie *The Parent Trap,* starring Dennis Quaid, Natasha Richardson, and a twelve-year-old Lindsay Lohan.[1] Our kids love this movie, and we were watching it for the twentieth time one night when Shaunti pointed out a perfect illustration for this book.

In the movie, two preteen girls realize they are twins who were separated at birth when their parents divorced. So they plot to get Mom and Dad back together by switching places. The British mom and American dad still care about each other, and when they finally meet again, Nick asks his ex-wife, Elizabeth, about what happened between them.

> NICK: It ended so fast.... So about that day you packed... why'd you do it?
>
> ELIZABETH: Oh, Nick. We were so young. We both had tempers, we said stupid things, and so I packed. Got on my very first 747, and...you didn't come after me.
>
> (Dead silence.)
>
> NICK: I didn't know that you wanted me to.
>
> ELIZABETH (smiling bravely): Well, it really doesn't matter anymore. So, let's just put a good face on for the girls and get the show on the road, huh?

Shaunti said this was an example of where the woman really *wanted* the man to come after her.

I asked, "But why didn't she just *tell* him that she wanted him to stop her from leaving? Why play games and make him read her mind?"

She looked at me, totally astonished. "Because if she said 'Come after me,' it wouldn't *mean* anything! It would be her decision, not his. She'd always doubt whether he did it on his own or because she asked him and guilted him into it."

Oh. Now I get it.

The movie, by the way, ends well. Nick finally realizes that, in spite of Elizabeth's seeming to push him away, she still wanted him to follow. And so he does. Because he learns to pursue, learns to reassure, the family is reunited.

Chances are, your wife or girlfriend is carrying around an unseen uncertainty about your love and needs you to come after her, look her in the eye, and tell her that you love her…and you're not going to let her get away.

Reassurance

3

WINDOWS...OPEN!

*What you should know about
the fabulous female brain
(a guide for lower life forms)*

*Women deal with multiple thoughts and emotions
from their past and present all the time, at the same
time—and these can't be easily dismissed.*

ne day early in our research, my kids and I dropped by the home of some close friends, Alec and Susie. While our children played outside, Alec asked me what I'd been learning about the mysterious other gender. I tried to describe a growing realization:

The female brain is not a normal instrument.

Normal, Alec and I agreed, would mean *male*.

Instead, I described what many women had told me: that their thought lives were like busy computers with multiple windows open and running all at once, unwanted pop-ups intruding all the time, and little ability to close out or ignore any of that mental or emotional activity until a more convenient time.

My friend shook his head in amazement. Strange, we both agreed. Very strange.

> Women's thought lives are like busy computers with multiple windows open and running all at once.

Susie, sitting at a nearby computer, had been listening, much amused, to the male sleuths at work in her kitchen. So my friend and I decided to test my working conclusions on the spot.

"Okay, hon," said Alec, "what is in your brain *right now*?"

She looked up. "Right now? Well, let's see." She started ticking things off on her fingers. "I'm thinking about all the points I want to make in this article I'm writing. I'm thinking I need to check the pizza in the oven pretty soon. I'm hoping the kids are doing okay out on the trampoline and that I should check on them. I'm wondering whether we're going to hear back tonight on this business deal we're waiting on. And I'm thinking about what I can say to move things forward."

She hesitated a moment, then looked back up at Alec. "And if you really want to know, I keep worrying about the argument you and I had this morning, and whether you're still upset."

He and I looked at each other, stunned.

"There's probably more," she said. "You want me to keep going?"

Alec said what any guy would be wondering: "How do you get anything done with all that stuff in your head?" And more to the point, "Why don't you just turn off all the other thoughts so you can concentrate?"

Susie looked perplexed. "Because I can't," she said. "And even if I did, they'd come back."

> This female multitasking of thoughts and feelings impacts how your wife or girlfriend relates to you every single day.

After hearing this sort of thing dozens of times, I realized that how a woman multitasks her thoughts and feelings isn't just an interesting academic difference between the sexes. It probably impacts how your wife or girlfriend relates to you every single day. That means a closer look at this mysterious mental difference is definitely in order.

Emotions

HER MYSTERIOUS MATRIX

Picture this: you're at your computer, moving among six or seven windows. Perhaps you're juggling three or four Word documents, an Excel spreadsheet or two, and your home budgeting program. Your e-mail program and Internet browser are running in the background, and your computer is playing your favorite webcast radio program. It's a digital Grand Central Station.

Now imagine that some of the files and programs have been open and running in the background for weeks. Even worse, your computer is infected with spyware that causes annoying advertisements to pop up. You've tried to close these unwanted files and pop-ups many times, but they just keep coming back. The best you can do is to minimize or ignore them so you can focus on the other half-dozen tasks you're actively juggling at any one time...

Welcome to a woman's mental and emotional world—a world that has probably affected yours more than you realize. Here's what our surveys found:

1. Most women juggle multiple thoughts and feelings at the same time.
2. About half of all women have stored thoughts or feelings from the past that regularly pop up into active mode *whether they want them to or not.*

3. Women seem consistently unable to close these windows and "just not think about it" as easily as men can.

Let's look more carefully at what each of these statements means, how this affects you, and how to make the most of the mysterious but wonderful way your wife or girlfriend is wired.

Women seem consistently unable to close these windows as easily as men can.

THERE'S A LOT GOIN' ON IN THERE

Take multitasking. I've suggested that, like a computer running multiple programs, my wife tends to have many different thoughts and feelings running in her brain all at the same time. Where I would tend to process thoughts and feelings sequentially—working on one window at a time, closing it, and moving to the next— Shaunti is likely to have many windows open simultaneously and is able to jump back and forth among them at will. Or against her will.

In fact, on our survey, nearly eight out of ten women described themselves in similar ways. Agreement became almost universal (in the 90–95 percent range) for women under forty-five and those with middle-school or younger children at home.

Emotions

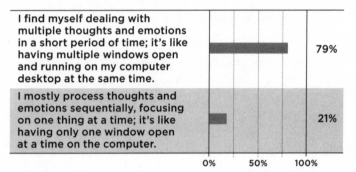

Which scenario best describes how you experience thoughts and emotions? (Choose one answer.)

I find myself dealing with multiple thoughts and emotions in a short period of time; it's like having multiple windows open and running on my computer desktop at the same time.	79%
I mostly process thoughts and emotions sequentially, focusing on one thing at a time; it's like having only one window open at a time on the computer.	21%

To be honest, most guys I know would be tempted to conclude that women clearly have major processor problems (to stick with the computer analogy). To our way of thinking, *their* way of thinking needs a fix!

But that's not the case. Interestingly, new research continues to show that a woman's brain is fundamentally different from a man's brain, and it doesn't need fixing—we just need to understand how it works. The fact is, every behavior I've described so far in this chapter can be traced in large part to the unique way her brain is wired.

Peeking into Her Brain

We've learned about some pretty interesting brain science since we published the original edition of this book—brain science that shows that women aren't *trying* to have all these open windows any more than we're trying to have just one open at a time. Women are simply designed this way.

Here's the main thing you need to know: a key reason for all these female windows is the ratio of gray matter to white matter in the corpus callosum superhighway between the hemispheres of a woman's brain.[2] Essentially, gray matter is like the computing power of the brain (where the actual processing and functioning is done) while white matter is like the network cables that connect the computers for speed, allow them to work together, and send signals from one computer to the next. Well, women have more white matter in their brain's superhighway than we do; while men have more gray matter. Neither is better or worse, but each leads to different ways of working through thoughts and emotions.

In practical terms, what does this mean?

Women's brains are designed specifically to process a lot of different things quickly, all at the same time—to be working on all those windows simultaneously—while men's brains are designed specifically to process deeply one thing (one window) at a time without being distracted.

What It Looks Like on the Outside

Although a woman's wiring may seem foreign to us, think how the unique properties of the female brain prepare her in so many ways for success. Think, for example, of how you've watched in

Emotions

amazement as your wife or mom managed an onslaught of cranky kids, made dinner, talked on the phone to a colleague, and let the cat out…all at the same time. Think of how her brain has nurtured countless relationships, done the advance work to arrange play dates, activities, birthday parties, and summer camps, or deftly managed the web of commitments in an extended family while holding down a job outside of the house. You get the idea.

Because of our brain's wiring, of course, most men are different. I have compared notes with a lot of guys, and to a man, we all get a charge out of the feeling of going into "the zone" and thinking deeply about one thing with absolutely no mental distractions—a sensation that perplexes most women when I describe it.

> "There's never a time that there's nothing going on in my head."

Of course, we men love having no windows open at all. Early in our marriage, if Shaunti found me sitting by myself, she'd ask me what I was thinking. When I answered, "Nothing," she'd get irritated and press me to *please* tell her what I was thinking. She didn't understand that I really was thinking about nothing! My desktop was empty, a screen saver was up, and no one was home.

Do you relate? Women don't. As one woman emphasized,

"There's never a time that there's nothing going on in my head. If I answer 'nothing,' it's because I'm mad at him!"

INVASION OF THE POP-UPS

Not only do women have multiple thoughts running all at once, about half of all women regularly experience uninvited thoughts, worries, or feelings—from the present or the past—that pop up and interrupt their day. For the men who live with them, that means they often interrupt ours too!

With their particular brain wiring, a woman is more likely than a man to be hit with unresolved concerns from something that happened last night, last month, or ten years ago. It might seem that she's choosing to dwell on something that's better left alone—even choosing to irrationally rehash or return to a matter that he thought was closed. But for her it's not irrational. In fact, since this is the way she's wired, it would be irrational for her *not* to address something that has circled back around.

According to our national survey, about half of all women are interrupted by these pop-up thoughts or feelings multiple times a week, even multiple times a day. Among younger women and those with children at home, the proportion was higher: 55–60 percent of survey takers. Perhaps not surprisingly, the percentage rose as high as 80 percent among women who described their relationship as shaky and those in difficult financial straits.

Emotions

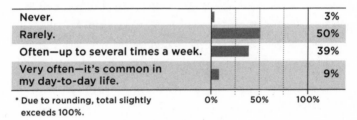

Some women say that emotions from experiences in the recent or even distant past (particularly negative ones) sometimes rise up in their minds. These may be triggered, or may seem to arise from nowhere. How often do you experience this? (Choose one answer.)

Never.	3%
Rarely.	50%
Often—up to several times a week.	39%
Very often—it's common in my day-to-day life.	9%

* Due to rounding, total slightly exceeds 100%.

It's not that women are helpless victims of these mental and emotional intruders. They're just more likely than men to experience them and to have difficulty getting rid of them. One woman in a focus group put it this way: "A lot of women will say, 'Don't play that tape in your head. You have to stop. Stop, don't go there with that thought.' It's easier said than done, but at least we try."

Actually, We Do This Too...

Does that comment sound startlingly familiar to you? I realized that we men can understand this struggle intimately because we have a visual parallel. Every man knows what it is like to have tempting, unwanted images pop up in his mind. In fact, this also is due to our different brain wiring. Our memory circuits as men are more tied to the things we see—so we're far more likely to have pop-up visuals. A woman's memory circuitry is more tied to language and emotions, so she is more likely to have pop-ups about her feelings and what has transpired in a relationship. As one woman wrote,

> If all men are truly visual and can't help it, then I think they should please understand that women are truly verbal and can't help it. For example, the things men say to us are in mental tape archives and are as real today as they were the moment they were spoken.

▶ "The things men say to us are in mental tape archives and are as real today as they were the moment they were spoken."

So That's Why...

The involuntary, long-term nature of this can help explain why more than one husband has felt:

- blindsided when his wife brings up something that happened two years ago.
- surprised by a sudden flareup of emotion attached to a memory.
- stung by unexpected heat that turns a conversation into an argument.

Emotions

- annoyed when a woman jumps topics in a conversation.
- dismayed that his wife got hurt by something seemingly outside the moment's mood or context.

If you're like me, you might think that she is unwilling to let go of something—an old offense or memory or grudge. Or that she's choosing an emotional response instead of a rational one—as if the two were mutually exclusive. (Hint: for women, they're not.) What's more likely is that some unwanted concern is invading her mind—an old problem that has never really been resolved or healed. Or some current trouble keeps invading her awareness—an open, running window that keeps painfully popping to the fore even if she doesn't want it there. If an unwanted concern is invading her mind, her emotional reaction is a reasonable response.

> If an unwanted concern is invading her mind, her emotional reaction is a reasonable response.

WHERE'S THE CLOSE BUTTON?

And that brings us back to the most important insight for this chapter: because of her brain wiring, the woman in your life finds it difficult or impossible to close out and ignore unwanted thoughts and feelings. These unwanted intruders are simply there until whatever is causing them is resolved in some way.

We've all heard that women don't compartmentalize like we do, but I never before understood what that meant. To illustrate, let's go back to the conversation in Alec and Susie's kitchen. I, too, had several things on my mind, including that I should check on the kids in the backyard. But when I compared notes with Shaunti, we realized that I handled those thoughts much differently than she could have in the same situation.

JEFF: I'm talking with Alec and thinking, *Should I check on the kids? Yeah, I'll do that in about five minutes.* Then I simply put it out of my mind—like on a five-minute mental timer. I don't give it another thought until the timer goes off.

SHAUNTI: How do you *do* that? I would love to put a thought on a timer and not think about it, but it's impossible. I simply have to function around that awareness that the kids need to be checked on or my friend is having a hard time with her marriage and needs me to call her or whatever. It never really goes away until the issue is resolved.

Of course, when I told Shaunti my timer function could actually put an issue that I didn't want to deal with on hold and out of mind for *weeks*, her interest in my brain turned to alarm.

Emotions

> The vast majority of women just aren't wired
> to easily ignore unwanted thoughts.

Our survey shows that the vast majority of women just aren't wired to easily ignore unwanted thoughts. As one woman said, "The best I can do is to 'minimize' the other windows, not close them. I'm not actively thinking about those things every minute, but they aren't gone either. And they often pop back up and become active when I don't want them to."

On those occasions when you have multiple emotional "windows" open, how readily can you usually dismiss negative thoughts and emotions that are bothering you? (Choose one answer.)

I can do it easily.	19%
I can do it, but it takes effort.	22%
I can do it with effort, but those thoughts/feelings sometimes pop back up until whatever is causing them is resolved.	36%
I usually can't dismiss them entirely; until whatever is causing them is resolved, those feelings are "open" and running in the background.	23%

0%   50%   100%

For more than four out of five women, closing out their unwanted thoughts either required effort or was impossible. The vast majority indicated that those thoughts would never really go away, or would at least keep returning, until whatever was causing them was resolved.

Which means our usual manly advice "Just don't think about it" is about as helpful as another shovelful of sand in the Sahara.

WE CAN RELATE

Here's a way that you can almost certainly relate to what this feels like. Imagine that your company just lost its biggest client, and at 5:00 p.m. on Friday your boss says, "I need to see you in my office first thing Monday morning." If you're like me, your weekend is ruined and anxious thoughts wreak havoc until Monday arrives. Your normal ability to compartmentalize is compromised by the magnitude of the concern.

Women aren't that dissimilar; it's just that their magnitude threshold is far lower than ours. Just as you couldn't close out anxious thoughts about what might happen on Monday morning, she can't close out all sorts of open windows.

That gives you a glimpse into how your wife feels when you have a bad argument in the morning and are at odds with each other. You can usually go off to work and put it out of your mind, but she may be completely unable to do that. The awareness that something is wrong stalks her thoughts all day—until you reassure her, "We're okay." Once you do that, even if the argument

Emotions

itself isn't resolved, she can usually take a deep breath of relief. (See chapter 2 for why.)

> You can usually go off to work and put an argument out of your mind, but she may be completely unable to do that.

DINNER WITH BOB AND DONNA

I think we men need to have our eyes opened to the real-life examples all around us so we can see how this actually works and know what to *do* about it. So let me pick an example that happened while Shaunti and I were in the middle of writing this chapter.

Shaunti was out of town with the kids, and a colleague invited me over for dinner with him and his wife, Donna, and their two small children. When I arrived, Bob was working in another room with one of those fire-starter devices that you click to get a flame. The following conversation occurred as the adults sat down for dinner a few minutes later.

DONNA: Honey, what did you do with the fire starter?
BOB: I left it in the other room.
DONNA: But…the kids are in there.

BOB: It's okay. It would be impossible for them to
figure out how to get a flame—it's pretty difficult
to use.

DONNA: But what if—

BOB: Really, hon, there's no way they would be strong
enough to click the flame on.

DONNA: Okay... That's true...

Previously, I wouldn't have thought a thing about this con-versation. But now, as I watched Donna across the table, I could tell—with my newly acquired supersensitive male radar—that a window had popped open and was not going to close until something set her mind at ease. So I mentioned to Bob and Donna what I'd been learning about how women couldn't usually just *decide* to close a window and not think about something that was bothering them.

Donna sat bolt upright. "That's it!" she said. "That's exactly what I'm feeling." She pushed away from the table, moved the fire starter out of the kids' reach, and came back.

"Now," she said, "I can enjoy dinner."

Bob and I realized that if she hadn't been encouraged to take that ten-second action, she would have been distracted and un-able to truly relax and enjoy the next hour of dinner. Even though she acknowledged that Bob was almost certainly correct that the

Emotions

kids couldn't ignite the fire starter, the window would have been open and bugging her.

> If she hadn't been encouraged to close that window, she would have been unable to relax and enjoy dinner.

I hope you see all sorts of ramifications of this female wiring. It explains:

- *why she seems preoccupied by "little things"*—even if you tell her to just ignore them.
- *why she seems to have been stewing over an argument*—or seems (to your male mind) to feel overly insecure about a disagreement you'd already dismissed or forgotten.
- *why she seems not to trust your decision*—or seems not to respect that you thought something through (for example, that the kids were too little to get past the child safety design of the fire starter).
- *why she might be too tired or upset for sex*—one woman put it this way, "Try to understand, we're carrying around *a lot* that we need to get out of our heads before we can really even feel like sex."

I don't know about you, but I don't even *need* my head to feel like sex.

SEQUENTIAL STRATEGIES FOR SEQUENTIAL MINDS

What's the average taken-aback man to do?

The good news of this chapter and this book is that a little understanding can go a very long way. It turns out that when you are confused by a concern that is bugging the woman in your life, taking a few ultrasimple action steps will usually bring immediate benefits to you both.

Remind Yourself: She Can't "Just Not Think About It," and That Fact Is Painful to Her

Let's say a pop-up of an old hurt from something you said has arisen involuntarily in your wife's mind, and she's having trouble closing it. Or maybe it's more recent: the two of you had words this morning, she knows you are angry, and her "Are we okay?" insecurity has been triggered.

Perhaps, though, it has nothing to do with you. Maybe she's unable to get a conflict with her boss off her mind. Or she's simply bugged by the thought, *Did I close the garage door when we left?*

Remember that because it's hard for her to just push something out of her mind, there's a risk she'll live in a marginally unhappy state for hours or, for the big concerns, days until her concern is addressed and hopefully resolved. Thankfully, you can play an important part in resolving it!

Emotions

Use Her Pop-Ups as Your Trigger to Help Her Close Those Windows

Here's what most men don't see as an opportunity—and where you now move from Average Joe to GI Joe. The next time you want to say "Just don't think about it" or "Don't worry about it, honey," stop yourself and realize, *This is my chance to earn major points.* Do as follows:

> ▶ *If the concern involves you and the relationship, listen and reassure.*

Now's the time to step up and help her close that window by giving her a listening ear, a hug, or the reassurance she needs so she can let go of any insecurity and resolve it in her mind. In particular, remember that if she brings up old wounds, she may not be holding on to a grudge but actually trying to process it so she can resolve it, close the window, and let it go.

> She may not be holding on to a grudge but actually trying to process it so she can let it go.

In any of these cases, you can help by letting her—actually encouraging her to—process these things the way she probably needs to: by talking it through and having you listen. (Note to self: *If I'm smart, I'll ask if she's okay well before bedtime.*)

▶ *If it doesn't involve you, listen and encourage her to take some action—or take it for her.*

It is astounding how loved it makes your wife or girlfriend feel when you encourage her if she needs to take some action to close her open window so it doesn't keep coming back. For example, "Would it help to call the Fosters across the street so they could check if our garage door is down?"

If it's an emotional problem (she's at odds with her boss or a close friend), part of helping her close the window means listening for a few minutes. But if your wife then keeps worrying out loud, "I'll bet my friend misunderstood me and is really upset with me right now. Maybe I should call her tonight." She will feel loved if you avoid the usual male line—"Ah, I'm sure it's fine. You can talk about it with her in the morning." Instead, simply say, "You know, honey, it sounds like calling her might make you feel better. Do you want to do that?"

Even better, take some action yourself. Get up from the dinner table, get her the fire starter, and say, "I wanted to be sure you could enjoy dinner without worrying."

Try it. Be one of the few, the proud, the in-the-know heroes.

Emotions

4

THE REASON HIDING IN HER "UNREASONABLE" REACTION

How you can actually break the code of baffling female behavior

> *There is usually a logical reason behind her baffling words or actions—and behavior that confuses or frustrates you often signals a need she is asking you to meet.*

Y ou sit at the computer keyboard and hit the *q* key, and it works. The letter *q* appears on your screen. Hit the same key again, and there it is again. The same *q*. Every time. No fuss. No variation.

Hit *q*, get *q*. Hit *q*, get *q*. Input equals output. *Ahhh!* In that predictability and order, a man finds comfort. And thankfully, this is how business, technology, barbecues, and the television remote work. Pretty much, anyway.

And then there's the woman you love.

Your experience with her, we're guessing, looks more like this: Hit *q*, get *q*. Hit *q* again, get...*4*?

You're thinking, *This worked, this worked... What happened here?* Ever since Cro-Magnon days, men have been sure of just one thing about women: on a regular basis—and usually when you least expect it—women will stop making sense.

You think you're talking about changing the oil in the car. Out of nowhere, she wants to know if you think her sister is still mad at her. As you pull into Oil Changes to Go, she's now mad at *you* for forgetting to tell her that her sister called.

You think the restaurant is fine. Out of nowhere, she says you just don't care anymore.

You thought you had a great evening together. Out of nowhere—or so it seems to you—she puts on flannel pajamas and turns in for the night.

All too often, we think, there's no rhyme or reason behind her reactions. Or if there is a reason, we're sure we'll never be able to understand it. Clearly, the only sensible thing is to throw up our hands and try to ignore the problem. We leave her alone until she calms down, hoping it will get better on its own.

Here's the thing, though. With a computer you'd never do that. You would reboot, try to figure it out, call a help desk. You'd never just ignore it.

Why the difference? It's not because you really love the computer and don't care as much about the woman in your life. It's always the other way around. (And if it's not, you've got bigger problems than are covered in this book, my friend.)

No, the reason for the difference is that with the computer *you know there's a reason things aren't working.* And you assume it can be fixed, so you take a crack at it.

Imagine my shock when I discovered that the same thing holds true for women.

CLUES TO THE CODE

I'm not a literature guy, but I once saw a quote by Oscar Wilde: "Women are meant to be loved, not to be understood."

That pretty much sums up our mental default setting ever since Cro-Magnon man proudly brought home a giant sloth for dinner, only to be met with a cold female stare because his hunting party got home two days late. Grunting whatever sounds meant "Fine!" he took refuge with the other bewildered hunters who had been tossed out by the communal fire for the night.

That also sums up the mental default setting most of us learned as teenagers. Nothing prepares you for that moment when

Decoding

you are thirteen—thrilled to be standing in the hallway with the cute girl you're crazy about—and suddenly something awful happens. Whereas yesterday she smiled at you like you were the middle school's Big Man on Campus, today she won't. She's upset. She's cold. She won't even look at you!

You're desperate to know what happened, what went wrong, but you don't have a clue. So you retreat to the locker room, lick your wounds, and joke that girls are impossible to understand.

We have to sweep up the little pieces of our ego somehow, right? As the years pass, a teen guy's feeling of cluelessness about girls morphs into a generally acceptable view among men that women are impossible. "Good luck trying to figure *her* out!" we say to each other in those moments of frustration.

Trouble is, we're setting ourselves up for one of the most damaging assumptions to a relationship we can make. Especially because it is totally wrong.

It turns out, a huge percentage of men have to unlearn what we think we know about the reasonableness of women. Because in our research, when a woman seems inscrutable or her attitudes, actions, feelings, or words change in confusing ways, there is almost always a specific, discernible reason—a reason that men would usually see as legitimate if we understood it.

And the truth is, we can—if we pay attention.

Believe it or not, even among those teenage girls who crushed our hearts with their unpredictable behavior, there are actual, board-certified reasons for what baffled us. Look how even the most hormone-riddled adolescent girls answered on their survey:

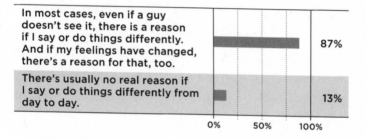

Many guys believe that there aren't really rational reasons when a girl's attitudes, actions, or words change from day to day. Which of the following is true of you? (Choose one.)

In most cases, even if a guy doesn't see it, there is a reason if I say or do things differently. And if my feelings have changed, there's a reason for that, too.	87%
There's usually no real reason if I say or do things differently from day to day.	13%

Almost nine out of ten girls emphasized that there is a reason for everything they do and say. Among the adult women we interviewed, the number was nearly 100 percent. Lest you think they are simply delusional, this was verified, in personal interviews and focus groups, by asking each time, "What was the reason?" and getting a well-thought-out answer that left the previously skeptical men in the room stunned.

In the last chapter we saw an example of this. We saw that even some of the weirdest displays of supposed randomness—such

Decoding

as when a female worry resurfaces "out of nowhere"—actually stem from the brain wiring of multiple mental windows running in the background.

In this chapter we take things further. We show that "female" and "illogical" don't actually go together as much as we thought, if at all. Perplexing behaviors aren't coming out of nowhere. Further, we'll show that once husbands and boyfriends decide to proceed on the assumption that (1) good reasons exist for her actions and (2) that we can discover and act on those reasons, our relationships will dramatically improve.

That's because those convenient (and centuries old) assumptions of randomness can actually prevent us from finding happiness with a wife or girlfriend—and from making her happy as well.

> Those old assumptions can prevent us from finding happiness—and making her happy too.

You see, when a confused husband frequently resorts to the "throw up his hands, retreat, and hope it gets better on its own" routine, real trouble can develop in his relationship, and he risks not seeing it coming. We have seen some heartbreaking survey responses where a man described his marriage as being at the happiest mark on the scale while the woman in the same relationship described the marriage as being "very unhappy." Ouch!

To be clear, we're not trying to put doubts in your head about your relationship. We just want you to know that the advice in this chapter is both important and full of promise. Because once you assume she can be understood, a good outcome is not only possible but likely.

Which beats being totally confused and ending up out by the fire with the other Cro-Magnons.

BREAKING THE CODE

As a starting point, when we see something that seems confusing, random, out of proportion, or completely nonsensical, we have to believe there's a reason for it—probably a legitimate reason. Work with me here, okay? I know that may seem as unlikely as the Detroit Lions making it to the Super Bowl (yes, it's been a long few decades for us Michiganders), but proactively choosing to trust that fact is essential. Once we do, we're ready to discover the reasons behind baffling female behavior. The women in our surveys offered four possible code breakers that can help us understand even their most "irrational" words, feelings, and actions.

Possible Reason 1: It's Something You've Done, Even If You Don't Realize You Did It

This troubling insight won't surprise you. Most of us learned it in the throes of our first white-hot, kindergarten romance. Out of

Decoding

nowhere (there's that phrase again), guys are to blame. Since then, when anything seems suddenly awry, we have learned to wonder, *What did I do?*

Of course, moments later we have moved on to the only possible conclusion. *Nothing. I did absolutely nothing wrong.* Or we do a quick gallop around the options and conclude that it is absolutely ridiculous for her to be upset. She's being irrational. Obviously. Time to throw up our hands!

Not so fast, hunter-gatherer.

The following is a real-life example that may help us see how something we do can cause the woman in our life to behave in confusing and "unreasonable" ways.

It's a Date

Marco and his wife, Krissy, decide to have a long-awaited date night. He's been traveling, and she's been working long hours, helping Marco's brother, John, and his wife in their family business. After weeks of not seeing each other much, the two agree it's time for some romance.

So they make a plan for Friday. She will arrange a baby-sitter for the kids, and they'll each get off work early so they can catch an early movie. Then they'll go to dinner, come back home, get the baby-sitter returned safely by 10:00 p.m. (as promised), and—Marco hopes—enjoy the fact that the kids are asleep.

Marco gets home from work a bit later than he hoped, so they have to rush to make the movie. Fortunately, Krissy is generally pretty easygoing, so she doesn't seem to mind.

The movie is great, and they both laugh a lot. After too many weeks of distance, they're really enjoying being with each other. They hold hands and share popcorn.

Then on the way to dinner, Marco remembers something. He needs to stop by his brother's house.

"Why?" Krissy asks. She looks startled.

"Well, John told me there's something he needs to show me. Something exciting for his business. It'll just take a minute." He looks over at his wife. "Uh, is that okay?"

"Sure. Okay. If you need to," she says.

They drive to his brother's house, which is a bit out of the way, where John shows Marco something he's excited about that is getting rave reviews. It dawns on Marco that his wife must already know all this, since she has been working on the project intensively with his brother. Still, he lets John know how pleased he is for him (and Krissy) and spends about twenty minutes talking before he sees it is 8:30 and says they need to get going.

As they drive away, Marco is in cheerful spirits,

Decoding

excited for his brother, and glad to be having such an enjoyable evening out with his wife.

"So where do you want to go to dinner?" he asks.

"I don't care," Krissy answers. "You pick."

Those words don't sound quite right.

"No, really," he says, trying to be thoughtful. "Let's pick a place you've been thinking about. This evening is for you."

"Oh, really?" she replies.

Okay, now, he's *sure* those words don't sound right. "Yes, of course!" he insists. But he suddenly feels like he's in deep weeds.

Silence.

He presses ahead. "Uh…is something wrong?"

"No, it's fine."

But he can tell it's not fine. What to do but onward into the weeds. "Go ahead and pick a place, sweetie," he says, reassuring her, and then adds a helpful detail. "I guess it should be closer to home, though, since Jessie has to leave at ten."

"Yep."

Marco and Krissy drive to a restaurant near their house, a place they've been to before and know is nice.

Silence all the way.

By now Marco's male brain is spinning. *What happened to my sweet, affectionate wife? What's she doing to our enjoyable evening?*

Then he starts to get angry. If she's upset because he took twenty minutes out of the evening to talk about work with his brother—work she's been a part of—that's completely unreasonable!

After a fifteen-minute wait, they're seated at the restaurant, and out of nowhere—really—an argument starts over something stupid. By now it's after nine, and the two of them are seriously irritated with each other. They both try to smile and make small talk, but the evening is ruined. As Marco hurriedly asks the waiter for the check so they can get home by ten, he's pretty sure that the evening won't be ending the way he had hoped.

Sure enough, his wife returns from taking the baby-sitter home, climbs into bed in her flannel night-gown—the one that might as well say "Keep Your Hairy Paws Off" in big letters—and settles down to go to sleep.

Talk about unreasonable, confusing, and random! Marco gets up and trundles downstairs to watch late-night TV. With every step, he's wondering, *What on earth happened?*

Decoding

If you and I put ourselves in this story, we can easily empathize with the unlucky husband. Obviously, his wife got upset because she was looking forward to time together, and the little side trip to his brother's house took time away from that. Too much time, as it turns out.

Really, we're thinking. *Ruin an evening over a silly twenty minutes?*

But let's look at the story—and our reaction—in a fresh light. If women do have logical reasons for their reactions, then we need to be open to the possibility that the unlucky husband in the story did something—more than one thing, actually—that legitimately upset his wife. He could have done something truly hurtful, even if he didn't intend to, and, while he's sitting alone in front of the television, still doesn't know what it was.

Krissy told us it would have made all the difference if her husband would have indicated that he realized he may have done something insensitive and then done something more: taken the steps to pursue her further rather than accepting her "fine" as the last word and driving in silence to the restaurant.

> Although we see "Is anything wrong?" as a thoughtful—and sufficient—way of finding out if there's a problem, many women don't see it that way.

Although we see the "Is anything wrong?" question as a thoughtful—and sufficient—way of finding out if there's a problem, many women don't see it that way. We'll explain why in a moment. But for a woman, the necessary (read that, "reasonable and logical") steps instead often look like this:

1. If she's upset, always assume that it could have been something you did (not that it always *is,* but assume it could have been).

2. Ask her to tell you if you did something to mess things up.

3. Assume that "I'm fine" is not her final answer, *unless she specifically seems happy again and isn't upset like you suspected.*

4. Pursue her—gently and persistently—until she lets you in and reveals what she's really feeling. For example, "I know you say things are fine, but I think maybe I hurt your feelings just now. Can you help me understand what I did?"

Don't believe me? Here's what Krissy told us her husband would have heard if he'd assumed her confusing behavior was because of something he did *and then* pursued her further to discover the reason behind the behavior. Now, pay attention, cave mates, because—as you're about to find out—Marco's wife had a *lot* more on her mind than he ever realized:

Decoding

Really, all I wanted from the date night was two good hours over dinner to catch up. We hadn't really seen each other in weeks. The movie was nice, but that wasn't the point. What I was most looking forward to was finally having a couple of good hours over dinner.

And it wasn't just to reconnect. I had been managing this big project for my brother-in-law and was so nervous about it, since I'd only been back in the workforce a short time. But when it started to get all these clients and such good reviews, I was so thrilled. I couldn't wait to surprise my husband with it. I had purposely not told him on the phone. I wanted to see his reaction and wanted to see that excitement on his face and see him be proud of me.

I know it's probably stupid to be upset, but when he drove all the way across town to see John, I knew that not only had we lost any chance of a good, long conversation over dinner, but I had lost my big surprise announcement. I'm probably overreacting because I'm tired, but it was just a double whammy, and I was really wishing he would have picked up on it instead of just charging right ahead.

And then the fact that he *didn't* pick up on it just made it worse. Like, when you realize that it's not really "fine," why wouldn't you just ask another question? We're

sitting there in frosty silence; clearly it's not fine! If you
would just say, "I didn't mean to, but I think I hurt
you—what did I do?" it shows me that you care about
me, that you're willing to deal with it if you did do
something wrong. *That one action* on his part would
actually help make it fine!

Truly, I've seen that once we know the real reason behind
seemingly random or confusing behavior, we often completely get
why our wife was upset.

Possible Reason 2: It's Not Necessarily About You—It's About a Hidden-from-You Emotional Need Inside Her

This reason is closely tied to the first one, but it's so important, I
want to dig further.

First, some background. In the reassurance chapter (chapter
2), we talked about the fact that even the most secure women are
plagued by insecurity running under the surface. It's a deep personal doubt that makes her question, "Does he really love me?"
and "Are we okay?" If that insecurity is triggered by conflict or
distance between you, she needs reassurance of your love. Unfortunately for us take-things-at-face-value males—and this is
where we get the most frustrated—in this situation your wife or

Decoding

girlfriend is likely to subconsciously pull back. Not because she needs space but because she is *desperately hoping you will follow.*

> She subconsciously pulls back, not because she needs space, but because she is desperately hoping you will follow.

We showed in chapter 2 that, rather than get frustrated that she's playing games or testing us or even being manipulative, we need to see her actions for what they are: a plea for reassurance.

One key type of reassurance is to pursue her when you think you might have done something wrong (Possible Reason 1, above), even if she isn't owning up to it yet. Go with your gut. If she's saying "fine," but you think it's not, or if she's insisting nothing's wrong, but you suspect something is, don't drop it just yet. As Marco and Krissy's story illustrates, be willing to ask another question.

You may think the whole thing is illogical, unreasonable, foolish (or less polite words to that effect). Join the club. When Shaunti did this kind of thing, I used to think, *No way I'm playing her games.* Eventually, though, I realized that to Shaunti, it wasn't a game. Her inner doubt was very real. I didn't realize it, hadn't intended it, but her behaviors were explained by a deep and very understandable emotional need: she was feeling distant or insecure about my love.

After I finally got it, what I had thought of as a test became my visible signal of her invisible need. My next move wasn't always easy, but it is simple: don't withdraw but ask more questions. Do so without defensiveness, so you prove to her you truly *want* to know the answer. I don't always do this right, but I try to say something like, "I feel like I screwed up. I'm sorry. Help me understand." Your willingness to own the problem releases her ability to get her hidden-from-you emotional need out where you can both deal with it.

> What I had thought of as a test became my visible signal of her invisible need.

Well, why don't they just tell us?!

Ever wonder why women don't just tell us they are feeling insecure? Or why they don't just tell us the real deal the first time we ask? Here's why. According to the vast majority of the women in our research, we've trained them not to. And we've done that by consistently getting defensive and angry when they tell us what they're feeling or when they answer our questions honestly the first time.

If you doubt that, ask yourself how you would react if you had been Marco and your wife answered your "Is something wrong?" with what she was *really* feeling? Think about it. She says, "I feel bad that you didn't think through the fact that this

Decoding

'short' trip to see John would take at least forty-five minutes or an hour away from our dinner. I'm upset that it didn't occur to you that I might know *exactly* what John wanted to tell you, and you didn't seem to care that I was really looking forward to a long dinner to catch up with you!"

Honestly, how would you respond? I'm guessing that most guys would feel surprised and stung by such criticism. Then we'd feel dumb. Then we'd get angry.

So, then, as the women in the focus groups put it, "Is it any wonder that we subconsciously hold back, to make sure that you *really* want to know before we give you the real answer?"

Oh. Yeah. That makes sense.

Possible Reason 3: It's Not About You— It's About Her Circumstances

Just like you have bad days, so does she. You get short with your wife or kids because you're just on edge, and it has nothing to do with them.

What do you need at those times? Well, you hope your wife won't react in kind, that's for sure. You need her to give you a little space to get your bearings. Or maybe you need her to let you take your Craftsman cordless and drill holes all over your boss's face. (Okay, drill holes all over some plywood scrap in the garage and just kinda *pretend* it's your boss.)

What you don't need is her taking it personally. You certainly don't need an escalation, getting all upset that you're all upset.

Ditto for her. Sometimes it's not us. First, as mentioned earlier, ask if you did something wrong. (You're a man. You would jump in front of a speeding eighteen-wheeler to rescue her. I *know* you can ask her if you did something wrong.) And if she sincerely reassures you that it's not about you, bring out the listening ear or a shoulder for her to cry on.

Possible Reason 4: It's Not About You— It's Hormones

Okay, I have to be delicate about this, but let's all acknowledge the obvious: for some women, there are a few days each month when the reason behind the supposed randomness is simply chemical and biological, not something she's trying to do.

One of my buddies (wise man that he is) worked out a great system to handle this with his wife. She suggested that he keep rough track of her, er, situation, and when he's confronted with something seemingly out-of-the-blue irrational, before he answers (or responds in kind), he will gently ask her a question to confirm his suspicion.

Now, this is a jokester couple, so she thinks it's funny when he asks, "Am I talking to my sweet wife Lori or Helga the crazed mutant?" But for you to find out what kind of proactive measures

Decoding

your Lori might suggest for the two of you, we suggest a gentle conversation on a day when Helga is but a distant memory.

YOU CAN UNDERSTAND HER AND MAKE HER HAPPY

We didn't have this subject in the original edition, but once men started reading *For Men Only,* we got e-mails saying, as one put it, "Your research and surveys were helpful—but realizing that there *is* actually a method to her madness, and that I can find it if I look closely enough is, by itself, the single most important thing I learned."

To help you process the insights in the chapter, we've embedded many to-do suggestions in the text. Here's a quick summary:

- Assume there is a legitimate reason behind what looks unreasonable to you.
- Take the time to gently and persistently pursue her to find out what it is. Listen to what she has to say without getting defensive or overreacting.
- Read those "illogical" behavior signals that cue when to step up as the Chosen Dude who can meet an important (previously hidden) need.
- Enjoy newfound bliss with the woman you love.

No matter how logical or linear you think you are, you can make the insights in this chapter work for you.

A friend of mine is an engineer (translation: trained to find solutions based on readily observable facts and formulas). He and his wife have a strong marriage, but he was at times confused and frustrated because he couldn't understand how seemingly small stresses and circumstances could overwhelm her and cause "irrational" anxieties.

On a recent flight, he was rereading *For Men Only* and began to consider what might be going on inside her during those anxious times. He wondered if it was comparable to certain things that had made him anxious.

So he wrote a letter and e-mailed it from the plane, wondering if those situations might be similar to what she regularly goes through. He ended the letter with "Does any of what I said relate to what you experience? Am I gaining an understanding of what you experience? I hope so. Not that any of this helps resolve anything. But at least you and I are closer because I understand what you go through…I hope."

How did she react to his letter? Here's her e-mail back to him:

As I sit here reading your letter, tears are streaming down my face. Thank you for caring enough to even try to "get" my thought processes. Thank you for never giving up on me as I go through episodes of anxiety. Just the thought of you taking the time to try to understand humbles me beyond words.

Decoding

As my friend's story shows, once you take the step to trust that the woman in your life is *not* an unreasonable alien that you'll never figure out, you can begin to take seriously the visible signals of her invisible inner life. Then, with a dose of courage and some sincere practice, you can do the seemingly impossible.

You can make her happy.

And—we know this, men!—that will make us happy too.

5

YOUR REAL JOB IS CLOSER TO HOME

How your provider/protector instinct can leave her feeling more unsafe and less cared for

> *Your woman needs emotional security and closeness with you so much that she will endure financial insecurity to get it.*

t happened the minute I decided that Shaunti was the woman I wanted to marry. As soon as I thought about accelerating our relationship...I stalled.

Most guys I've talked to can relate. All my forward momentum vanished as anxiety stopped me in my tracks. The issue wasn't her or how much I loved her or what I really wanted to happen between us—and soon. The issue was money. It suddenly hit home: how will I take care of a wife and provide for her financially? I didn't know much about relationship stuff, but I knew one thing: women want security.

> I knew one thing: women want security.

I grew up in a small farming community in Michigan and had known plenty of financial struggles in my life. After high school, I scraped by in the restaurant business for seven years before I went to college. But Shaunti was from the upper-middle-class suburbs of Washington, DC, and hadn't experienced similar struggles. I was concerned about what she would consider a normal standard of living and whether I could provide it. So I waited. With that in mind, when I graduated from law school, I took a job with a big New York law firm that included a very good salary.

Finally, I figured, I could provide. So we got married and moved into a doorman building in the heart of Manhattan. In New York, doorman buildings are common *and* pricey. But Shaunti preferred one because it made her feel more secure, she said.

Aha! I thought, confident in my manly insight into her needs. *Even if I might have preferred a different job, I'm doing what men do. I'm providing security for my wife.*

Then I proceeded to work eighty-hour weeks to pay for it all. During the next five years, whenever Shaunti said that I was choosing work over her or that I didn't care about her, I experienced a strong and predictable reaction—I got upset. *How can she accuse me of not caring about her when I am busting my tail to prove exactly that?!*

Recently, when I asked a friend what he thought "women want security" meant, he described a common male dilemma. "It means I can't ever stop running," he said. "I need to do whatever I have to do to *ensure* that she doesn't feel financially insecure. And if it means that I have to work really long hours or stick with a job that I don't like all that much, so be it."

Perhaps you, too, have felt caught between a rock and a hard place, knowing that your wife wants you to provide a nice life for her and the kids, but she also wants you home by dinner. Impossible financial expectations on her part?

Maybe. But probably not.

As you'll see in this chapter, men may be really frustrated by what they think their wives expect, but their wives may have no such expectations. In our case, it turns out the doorman building in Manhattan wasn't nearly as important as I'd thought.

Security

MONEY TALKS BUT EMOTIONAL SECURITY SINGS

Our research shows that, yes, women want security. But they mean something very different by it than we do. A woman's primary thought is not about a house, a savings account, or tuition for the kids. For her, *emotional* security matters most. As we'll discuss, this means that she feels emotionally connected and close to you and *knows* you will always be there for her, no matter what. Sure, providing financially is appreciated, but for most women it's nowhere near the top of their list.

In fact, as one woman told us, "It's not even on the same list! Feeling secure and close in the relationship is so much more important, it's not even part of the same discussion as work or money."

> When a woman thinks of security, her primary thought is not about a house, a savings account, or tuition for the kids.

Forgive my confusion. Yes, I heard Shaunti *say* she wanted more of me. But I also heard her say she wanted the doorman building. I assumed that she was choosing financial security over a saner and more enjoyable career for me. Her insistence that she wanted to make changes so I could be around struck me as appreciative gestures aimed at making me feel less pressured.

But now, I realize (a little late) that she actually *meant* it. And a lot of women feel the same way. On the survey, seven out of ten married women said that, if they had to, they would rather endure financial struggles than distance in the relationship.

Why don't you read that again. I know we find it impossible, but it's true: 70 percent of married women would prefer to be financially *insecure* than endure a lack of closeness with their husbands.

In fact, even single women showed the same preference. And women who described themselves as struggling financially were even *more* likely to prefer emotional security!

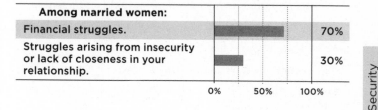

If you had to choose between these two bad choices, would you rather endure... (Choose one answer.)

Among married women:		
Financial struggles.		70%
Struggles arising from insecurity or lack of closeness in your relationship.		30%

Security

The problem here is that what seems blazingly obvious to women is barely visible for most men—or men simply don't believe it. One time, a male pastor was interviewing Shaunti on-stage in front of a large group of twenty-something singles. A few minutes in, Shaunti decided to test our emerging hypothesis on this issue. She turned to the women in the audience and asked our survey question: "If you had to choose, would you rather endure financial struggles or would you rather endure struggles arising from insecurity or a lack of closeness in your relationship?"

Nearly every female hand went up for the "I'd rather endure financial struggles" option.

Shaunti used that demonstration as a launching point and began outlining for the women how men think about providing. After a few moments, the moderator interrupted. "I'm so sorry, Shaunti," he said, clearly flustered. "Could we back up a bit? I'm still so...shocked by what I just witnessed that I'm not hearing a word you're saying!" Much to the women's astonishment, men around the arena were nodding in agreement.

Yet women have an incredibly hard time believing that *we* think that *they* think financial security would ever be so important. As one woman asked in a focus group, "How could any man ever think we'd choose money over him?" Another said, "So in essence you guys are thinking that we are materialistic— really, really materialistic—and that we'd choose *things* over your happiness?!"

Uh...yeah. I guess that is what we're saying. But apparently we're wrong. For once, being wrong is very good news. Not only does the woman in your life care far more about you than about anything you could provide, but she's also willing to sacrifice financially to have more *of you* and more happiness *for you*.

THE INNER LIFE OF MR. PROVIDER

Are you still skeptical? One reason this is so hard to accept may have nothing to do with a woman's wiring but with ours. Shaunti's research for *For Women Only* demonstrated that three-quarters of men are "always" or "often" conscious of their burden to provide—and most of us wouldn't have it any other way.

Guys can't just demote work to some corner of our life. What we do defines us. Most days, it *is* us. That means our sense of self-worth—and a lot of other feelings—are wrapped up in it. For example, working toward our family's financial security is an important way we show our love. It's not a big jump to then think that longer hours = more love. And we assume the woman we love knows it!

The problem, I found, is that she *doesn't* know it.

In fact, since what she wants is your time and attention (which creates emotional security), if you appear to give more time and attention to work, it appears that you are making work your priority. To her, that means she is *not* your priority. That choice leaves her feeling distanced and unloved by you—even if the main reason you're busting your tail is to show her your love.

> Since what she wants is your time and attention, if you appear to give more time and attention to work, it means that she is not your priority.

Thankfully, there's a solution to this dilemma. To begin with, if security doesn't mean what we thought it did, let's redefine what security does mean to our wives.

WHAT SECURITY MEANS TO HER

Since most guys would never think to put *emotional* and *security* together in the same sentence, what does such a foreign concept look like in practical terms? Here's what we learned:

1. She feels that the two of you are close.
2. She sees that you make time together a priority.
3. She sees your commitment to her.
4. She sees that you are active in the life of the home.
5. She sees you making an effort to provide (as long as that doesn't crowd out 1–4).

Let's briefly outline each of these.

1. She Feels Secure When You Feel Close

Creating a sense of closeness between the two of you is more important than anything else—to a woman, it is almost a synonym for emotional security. And I was encouraged to see that it was *so easy.*

For us guys, money in the bank helps us feel safe and successful. But for women, the currency that counts is more likely to be a strong sense of closeness or intimacy with their man. In other words, your wife wants to be your love *and* your best friend—to know that she is yours and you are hers.

Here's the surprise for us guys: living in the same house and even having sex doesn't necessarily mean that she feels close to you. Most married guys I know just assume a level of closeness. We share a house and a bed. How could we *not* be close?

> For women, the currency that counts is a strong sense of closeness or intimacy with their man.

But for our wives, proximity and sex do not equal closeness. Consider the following exchange from one focus group when we asked how women felt when men traveled away from home:

Q: Is the only cure for loneliness for him to be there?
A: Not necessarily. Anyway, it's very easy to be lonely when he is physically there.

So what builds closeness?

Much of what creates a sense of closeness are the little things that come along with being each other's (1) love and (2) best friend.

Closeness means that she feels you belong to and love each other.

Even small gestures convey love and build closeness in a way I never would have thought. And they are so doable. Shaunti puts it this way:

Security

It's not that the little things somehow make a difference. It's that the little things *are* the difference between feeling secure and loved or not. The big things don't do that as much. The romantic dinner is wonderful once in a while. But that doesn't come close to building the same feeling of being loved that comes when you reach for my hand in a parking lot or leave me a silly voice mail calling me a special nickname that's just between us.

Here's the thing, guys: I didn't used to do those things that much. But once I discovered that the little things were that important… Well, heck, those I can do!

> "The little things *are* the difference between feeling secure and loved or not."

Every woman will be touched by different little things. But thankfully, this isn't rocket science. In one focus group, we were talking about what makes women feel loved, when to my surprise, Shaunti began to describe a recent incident. We had been walking through a parking lot, and I put my hand on the small of her back to steer her through some rows of cars.

Hearing that, every woman in the room put her hand to her heart or clasped her hands together and sighed: "Awwww," "Oh, that's so sweet," "What a good guy." The other men in the room and I looked at each other in shock. Especially because at the time I'd been worried that Shaunti might get mad at me for "telling her what to do"—since that would have been my reaction in a similar situation!

Closeness means that she feels you two are best friends.

Being close doesn't mean that you are her best *girl* friend—expected to talk for hours—but it does mean that you two know each other better than anyone else. As one woman put it, "My sense of security with my husband doesn't just come from expressing my emotions, but from knowing his."

2. She Feels Secure When You Make Time Together a Priority

As you might imagine, another thing that makes her feel secure is knowing that, after God, she's your priority. Knowing that she and the kids come before your job and that *you care for her first,* even if you feel your job is what you do to care for your family. Of the many women who echoed this view, one wife put it like this: "We can have plenty of money stored away and be very secure financially, but if I'm not secure about whether I'm a priority for my husband, all that money doesn't mean much. But on the other hand, if I know that he is there for me, I can face any struggles financially."

Security

For us nuance-challenged men, here's a simplified summary of what "being a priority" usually means to her: it is the amount of time and attention you give her outside of traditional work hours (meaning, outside forty or fifty hours a week) compared to anything else. Since there are only a limited number of possible "together" hours in a day, she views every above-the-norm hour spent on your work or outside interests as coming directly from the few hours she expected to spend with you.

> "If I know that he is there for me, I can face any struggles financially."

A wife does *not* expect her husband to spend every off-the-job hour with her. But to feel emotionally secure, she can't feel that he's consistently choosing other time priorities over her. As one woman said:

My husband is a very good provider, dearly loves his family, and says I complete him in every way. But he rarely seems willing to spend one-on-one time with me or to share my life, yet he always has time for the guys. I know he also needs his friends, but this lack of *me* in his day-to-day life is causing a big drift in our marriage.

3. She Feels Secure When You Demonstrate Your Commitment

Your wife needs to feel, in the core of her being, that nothing will scare you away and that you will do whatever you need to do to ensure that nothing comes between the two of you. One woman put it perfectly: "I need to know that he will be there for me, no matter what. We have a good relationship, but I still need to *know* that he's not going anywhere—physically or emotionally."

One simple way to demonstrate commitment is to reassure her after conflict, as we talked about in chapter 2.

4. She Feels Secure When You Are Active in Parenting and the Life of the Home

Women feel secure when they see their husband choosing to be an active participant in the life of the home, even if it means re-working other priorities. Unfortunately, if a man isn't careful, his laudable drive to provide may prevent him from taking that active role in the life the couple set out to enjoy together.

Some wives we surveyed felt like they started out as a general partner with their husbands, but somewhere along the way they wound up as a sole proprietor. One wife said,

> While we're not wealthy, we have some good funds saved
> up. But my husband seems to feel like we're always on the

Security

verge of a problem, so he has to always get that extra client, that extra paycheck, even if it means being locked in his home office all night after dinner, with no time to play with the kids. Will he ever feel that we have enough? I appreciate having that cushion—but not when it hurts *us*.

Another, by contrast, explained why she felt so secure:

My husband is working hard, but I'm so grateful that he also recognizes that kids need a dad's presence as much as they need a mom's. So many of my friends are frustrated that they have to ask their husband to "baby-sit," as if the kids aren't his kids too. My husband is so wonderful about recognizing that, yes, he's tired, but so am I. And the fact that he'll play with the kids or manage the dishes really gives me the sense that we're all in this together.

Further, quite a few busy moms told us that simply being appreciated by their husbands also helped them feel very secure. Any hardworking guy can understand the security that comes from feeling appreciated.

Any hardworking guy can understand the security that comes from feeling appreciated.

5. She Feels Secure When You Do Make an Effort to Provide

Lastly, after all this discussion of finances not being a woman's top priority, you should know that the effort you make to provide for your family does add to a sense of emotional security, even if the results aren't bringing in the amount of money you assumed she wanted. Where guys focus on the results, our wife focuses on the effort—and the effort does make her feel loved as long as it doesn't crowd out the other elements of emotional security.

The women we talked to agreed that in the choice between financial insecurity and emotional insecurity, it's not that they would *enjoy* financial struggles, but they would prefer to *endure* them if they could get more of you. As one woman said, "Financial struggles, by definition, are difficult. But if I had to, I'd rather have them than lose him."

> "Financial struggles, by definition, are difficult. But if I had to, I'd rather have them than lose him."

Obviously, in all of this, we need to find a balance. You are designed to want to provide for your family, and women do appreciate that. None of us would want to use these findings about emotional security as an excuse to quit our jobs, sit on the couch for hours, and eat Cheetos. Not that there's anything wrong with Cheetos, but all things in moderation.

THEY WANT US TO BE HAPPY

One of our most encouraging findings was that, even though women truly wanted their husband to have a job where he worked less in order to have more of his time, they also wanted him to work less so that *he* could enjoy life more. A great deal of a woman's stress and insecurity comes from knowing that her husband is working long hours at a job that causes him stress just to provide a certain level of income. If there were another option, most women would choose a lower-stress, lower-income job that he'd enjoy, even if it meant going through financial insecurity.

On our survey, we asked women to choose between two different job scenarios. Again 70 percent said they'd rather their husband take a lower-paying job that would require financial sacrifices if it allowed more family time. And even more fascinating, the number appears to rise to 89 percent if they felt *he* wanted to make that choice (adding in those women who were neutral)!

And encouragingly, even though women want emotional security and closeness, we could find none who would want their husband to take a family-friendly job that would make him unfulfilled or unhappy in his work life. They knew there was no emotional security in that solution. As one wife put it, "Then I would just have a depressed man on my hands, and that would defeat the purpose!"

Put yourself in this scenario: Your husband/significant other has a very well-paying job that requires a lot of hours and emotional attention away from home. You enjoy a comfortable lifestyle and all the enrichment opportunities for the kids that come with it, but you and the children often do feel distant from your husband/significant other, and when you two are together there is often discord. Now suppose that your husband/significant other was offered a different job that he'd enjoy, that would allow much more time with family—but it would also mean a substantial pay cut and some lifestyle adjustments for your family. Which best describes your likely feelings in this scenario? (Choose one answer.)

Security

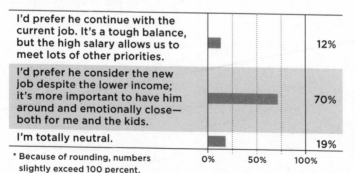

I'd prefer he continue with the current job. It's a tough balance, but the high salary allows us to meet lots of other priorities.	12%
I'd prefer he consider the new job despite the lower income; it's more important to have him around and emotionally close—both for me and the kids.	70%
I'm totally neutral.	19%

0%   50%   100%

* Because of rounding, numbers slightly exceed 100 percent.

RETHINKING OUR PROVIDER/ PROTECTOR ASSUMPTIONS

This whole topic boils down to asking ourselves—and asking our wives—one question: *Am I providing the type of security she genuinely wants and needs?*

One friend put his finger on the crux of the difficulty for many of us: "Men focus on income and possessions because it is so much easier to measure success in numbers. 'Loving attention' is much more difficult for us to quantify."

I started this chapter with the comment that we men often feel caught between a rock and a hard place. But we've now heard from hundreds of women that while there may be a rock on one side—her absolute need for emotional security—there is no hard place of absolute financial desire on the other. It's more like a *soft* place, since for most women all the money and things aren't nearly the priority that *you* are. Shaunti didn't want more of me *and* the doorman building. She wanted more of me, period. When I finally got that through my head—five years later—we moved from New York to a more family-friendly life in Atlanta.

If you suspect that perhaps your wife has been trying to say the same thing, have a talk. You might be surprised at what you hear.

> For most women all the money and things aren't nearly the priority that you are.

WHAT MATTERS: HAPPY DAD

We all instinctively know that as our children grow up and as we and our wives age together, our best memories will not center around the cool things we bought or the size of the house. Invariably, the measure of success will be something much simpler: the life we shared on a daily basis.

A woman who grew up in a large family in Flint, Michigan—one of those gritty industrial cities of the Midwest—described how more "providing" by her father had not turned out to be a better life for any of them:

Security

When we were little, we lived in a small house right in the city. The neighborhood wasn't great, but I loved my life. And my dad was a happy dad. When he was home from work, we'd all play. He was so much fun to be around.

When I was eleven, my dad wanted to provide a better future for us. So he decided to have a special home built outside of the city. Since we didn't have tons of money, he knew he'd have to do a lot of the work himself. He said we were worth it.

Unfortunately, he didn't realize what all the extra stress and pressure would do—not just to him, but to us. The stress of juggling everything began to wear my dad down. We lost happy dad and instead found grumpy dad. He stopped playing with us so much, and he was just on edge a lot, not relaxed and fun.

I now know that he was sacrificing himself to provide a better future for us kids, but we wanted *him* much more than we wanted the new house or better schools. We just wanted happy dad back.

She says that if the kids or her mom had been given the choice of the little home in Flint with happy dad or the bigger country home with grumpy dad, it would have been no contest. They all would have chosen happy dad.

◁ "We just wanted happy dad back."

A PERSONAL JOURNEY CLOSER TO HOME

Every guy I know who works hard does it at least in part because he believes he's doing what is best for his family. Providing for our family is commendable and a biblical injunction. But we must be willing to ask ourselves whether we are delivering what our family genuinely needs, or whether we have bought into some internal or cultural assumptions that might actually be sabotaging what matters most. If so, some adjustments are probably in order.

Looking back, I realize that my own dad *did* make those adjustments. My dad worked long hours in the unstable real estate business, but when he came home and there was any daylight left, we always threw the football around. Or he would hit fly balls to my brothers and me in the empty field beside our house. Good times.

> Because of my dad's presence in our lives, not a single memory centers on what we lacked. What I remember are the things we did together.

We always had a roof over our heads and three meals a day, but I do remember feeling the stress of belt-tightening measures during times when no commissions came in. But here's the thing: despite the pressures and despite knowing that we didn't have some of the things that other kids had, *because of my dad's presence in our lives* I have only amazing memories of my childhood. Not a single memory centers on what we lacked. What I remember are the things we did together.

Of course, cutting back financially to improve real quality of life does introduce its own stresses. Shaunti and I can attest to that. For several years, I struggled to keep a start-up technology company alive while developing a part-time legal practice. Many months we didn't know how we were going to pay the mortgage until it was due. Yes, that is stressful!

But we have managed, we've seen the truth that God always provides, and our family relationships are stronger than they've ever been. In fact, during one particularly tough financial season, Shaunti actually got *alarmed* when I floated the idea of going back to a big law firm. Honestly, I wouldn't trade the time I've been able to spend with Shaunti and the kids for any high-paying law firm job on the planet.

For men struggling with unemployment, job uncertainty, and tough economic times, it can be extra challenging to feel successful at home. Trust me, I know. You and I are wired to provide. When we can't, we easily fall victim to deep doubts about our worth as husbands and men. If you're facing this challenge today, I hope this chapter has convinced you that while you may sometimes feel like a failure, it does *not* mean your wife feels the same way.

To her, you are more than a paycheck. You mean more than the mortgage. You *do* hold the key to her sense of security, *especially* in hard times. But that security is not all about what you earn. It's about who you are—and how you love her—that counts most of all.

> You *do* hold the key to your wife's sense of security, *especially* in hard times. It's about who you are—and how you love her—that counts most of all.

Security

6

LISTENING *IS* THE SOLUTION

Why her feeling about the problem is the problem and how to fix your urge to fix

> *When she is sharing an emotional problem, her feelings and desire to be heard are much more important than the problem itself.*

Not long ago, Shaunti and I were cleaning up after dinner when I noticed that she seemed down. She had been working long hours on several projects, so I knew she was tired. She'd also just found out that an expected invitation to talk about *For Women Only* on CNN the next day had fallen through.

Supersensitive guy that I am, I probably would have stayed quiet and given her the space to work through it. But my recent work on mapping the female mind set me up to try something else. *She doesn't need space,* I realized. *She needs to talk.* So I paused, dish in hand, and asked if she was okay.

She sighed. "I'm just a little bummed about CNN," she said. "I know how networks work. I shouldn't have gotten my hopes up."

When I asked if she knew why it fell through, she shook her head. "Not really. They said everyone loved the topic, but when they got to the production meeting, some segments had to be cut. Nothing personal."

Since I really wanted to cheer her up, I decided the time was perfect to give Shaunti one of my best count-your-blessings pep talks.

"But, wow, think about what an amazing opportunity it is to even be in a position to be *considered* by CNN," I said.

"I know, but—"

"And think about what a blessing it is to be on *other* radio and TV all the time, to be able to share this message and save marriages."

"Yeah, but it's not the same as CNN."

"Oh, I don't know. You had five million viewers on that Hollywood talk show last month." I smiled. "That's a lot of people."

To my surprise, my reasonable, well-adjusted wife suddenly got angry. "I'm trying to tell you something, and you're acting like you don't even care!" She stood up from the table and seemed to be fighting back tears.

"Huh?" She'd really caught me off guard.

My mind started whirring. *You gotta be kidding me!* I thought. *You think I don't care? What do you think I've been trying to show you? That's the last time I try to encourage you!* But of course, I didn't say any of that. Instead, I muttered two tried-and-true gems: "Okay, fine." Then I shut down and went to see what was on TV.

Does this little scenario strike you as familiar? Here's the sequence again:

- She seems to need a listening ear.
- You care, so you say, "What's up?"
- She reveals what's bugging her.
- You care, so you try to help.
- She reacts with, "Obviously you don't care!"

Later, Shaunti and I both apologized. And we were able to identify the problem in our scenario: apparently, what I thought was listening and caring, wasn't. Of course, I *was* listening—using my ears, my brains, my stunningly good intentions. Really.

Trouble is, it just wasn't happening in the way that *felt* like listening and caring to my wife.

> Apparently, what I thought was listening and caring, wasn't.

Now that I've seen the massive response to this issue from women around the country, I believe that learning to listen in the way women need is a huge missing-in-action skill for most guys. If you're at all like me, the issue is complicated by more bad news— you already think you listen well. Heck, you think you're a listening machine—a real superman of sympathy! Most men do. I did.

Chances are, though, we're not.

But there's good news. Men might be broke down on this issue, but we're also just a few steps away from listening habits *that actually work,* which is what this chapter will show you.

Whether it's with your girlfriend or your wife, listening to her so she actually *feels* listened to will pay immediate dividends in a deeper, stronger, more rewarding relationship. Why? Because smart listening tells a woman louder than almost anything else that she is known, cared for, and loved. It's probably not too far off to state that smart listening has more power in her life and heart than—get this—all the things guys do first and best. Like analyzing, rescuing, deciding, doing, helping—or fixing the problem.

> Listening to her so she actually *feels* listened to will pay immediate dividends in a deeper, stronger, more rewarding relationship.

"SHE DOESN'T WANT YOU TO FIX IT"

We've all heard, "She doesn't want you to fix it. She just wants you to listen." But even though that phrase is accurate (according to all our interviews), most guys have no idea what it means or how to do it. I'll explain *how* in a minute, but first here's what it means. Three things:

- *She doesn't want you to fix it* = She doesn't actually want or need your solution to the problem—at least at the beginning.
- *She just wants you to listen* = She does want and need you to understand how she's *feeling* about the problem.
- *It* = an emotional problem. This listening rule does not apply to technical conundrums.

Let's take these one at a time.

"She Doesn't Want You to Fix It" = She Doesn't Need You to Fix It

In case you're wondering, this doesn't mean "she needs you to do nothing." Instead, the key is to understand *why* she's sharing something. And it's not—as we think—because she needs our help. In fact, our women usually feel quite capable of solving their problems without any help from manly men like us. That's not what they are looking for—at least at first.

Look at the results from the survey. Even if a man provided a very reasonable solution to the problem under discussion, just 5 percent of women said that would actually solve their problem. Add it up, guys. An enormous 95 percent of women feel that a reasonable solution would *not* solve their problem.

Suppose you had a fairly serious conflict with someone important to you, and have been dealing with strong emotions about it all day. That evening, you start to tell your husband/significant other what happened and how you feel about it. After listening for a little bit, he jumps in with a reasonable suggestion for fixing the problem. How is this most likely to make you feel? (Choose one answer.)

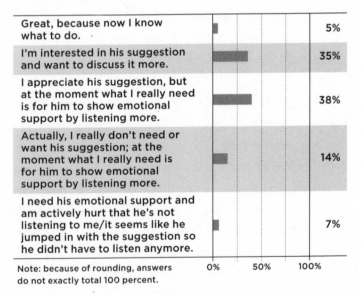

Great, because now I know what to do.	5%
I'm interested in his suggestion and want to discuss it more.	35%
I appreciate his suggestion, but at the moment what I really need is for him to show emotional support by listening more.	38%
Actually, I really don't need or want his suggestion; at the moment what I really need is for him to show emotional support by listening more.	14%
I need his emotional support and am actively hurt that he's not listening to me/it seems like he jumped in with the suggestion so he didn't have to listen anymore.	7%

Note: because of rounding, answers do not exactly total 100 percent.

0%   50%   100%

What's more, fully 60 percent of the women felt the offered solution—no matter how reasonable—was a negative. Some appreciated their man's suggestion, some didn't, but the majority felt that it detracted from the sense that he was listening and being supportive.

To see why this is true, we turn to the second and most important principle.

"She Just Wants You to Listen" = She Wants You to Focus on Her Feelings, Not the Problem

She's not sharing something so you can fix it. She's sharing it so you can understand how she *feels* about something that is bothering her.

Here's the thing: for most of our lives, we men have trained ourselves to cut through the clutter of emotion in order to focus on the "real issue." Instead, we need to grasp the single most important key to being a good listener: for a woman, her negative feelings about a problem *are* the real issue. In other words, her *feelings* are what she is trying most to share and have understood, even more than the problem itself.

> We have trained ourselves to cut through the clutter of emotion in order to focus on the "real issue." But for her, those feelings *are* the real issue.

Her need to get her feelings heard explains something that has confused many of us: *If she doesn't want me to fix it,* we wonder, *why does she keep talking about it?* Look at these revealing comments from women:

- "Most men feel they have to fix areas of concern for the wife and family. But when he jumps in before I am finished, he proves he isn't interested in listening to something that is important to me. This leaves me feeling devalued."

- "A few days ago, I was telling my husband about a longstanding relationship tension I have with someone. It was so sweet that he just listened, showed me his concern, and said, 'I don't know if it's going to get better, honey.' I felt so heard."

- "Just being able to share what's going on *actually fixes* something for a woman!"

> "Just being able to share what's going on actually fixes something for a woman!"

"It" = An Emotional Problem, Not a Technical One

The "she doesn't want you to fix it" mantra has confused many of us because we know some situations *require* a fix. Here's the difference: If it's an area of emotional concern, apply listening skills. If it's not, apply fixing skills.

Apply listening skills to areas that define a woman's relationships, well-being, and sense of self-worth. Home stresses, for example. Work. Friendships. Conflicts.

You.

This simply doesn't apply to those times when your wife tells you something is starting to howl under the gearshift in her Toyota. In such cases, you can safely forget her feelings—as in, "Honey, how does that make you feel when the transmission does that?" Just go male and fix away to your heart's content—as in, "I'll take it in to the shop tomorrow."

If you are ever confused about what the situation requires, women suggested that a guy just ask, "Sweetheart, do you want my help or do you just want me to listen?"

For any man who wants to be a good listener, the good news is that we don't have to shut off our Mr. Fix-It nature. We just have to apply those skills to the right problem—and in the right order. Let me assure you, this is a skill worth learning!

HOW TO LISTEN

As any guy at his workbench knows, sequence matters. And so it is with listening. Because the key to listening in the way a woman will feel heard is for us Mr. Fix-Its to fix it in the correct two-step order:

> Step 1: You ignore the problem and listen to her
>   feelings about it.
> Step 2: You sit down together and focus on the
>   problem.

Get them in the right order, and the woman in your life will be beaming. Do them in the wrong order, and—trust me on this—you'll hear, "But, honey, you're not *listening* to me!"

> The key is for Mr. Fix-It to fix it in the right order. Get the order right, and the woman in your life will be beaming.

Step 1: Ignore the Problem and Focus on the Feelings

The reason many women think we don't listen is that, when it comes to an emotional issue, we aren't necessarily listening for the right things. Our definition of listening is often a bit more basic. Something like, "She's talking, and *I'm hearing what she's saying*—therefore, I'm listening."

But look at those italicized words and realize something: she does not want you to hear what she's *saying;* she wants you to hear what she's *feeling.* So the first and most important step for Mr.

Fix-It is to listen for the right thing: how she *feels* about the emotional issue she's bringing to you.

Most of us feel like all those jangling emotions will only get in the way of clear thinking and addressing the problem properly. So we try to filter them out. We don't realize that what we are so busy filtering out is what she most wants us to listen to!

In Step 1, we need to retrain ourselves to do something that will feel very weird at first: filter out the problem and instead focus on those jangling feelings about the problem. In fact—and I know this might be a scary thought!—we need to purposefully investigate and pull out those feelings to help her work through them.

> We need to retrain ourselves to filter out the problem and focus on all those jangling feelings about it.

In the CNN example, Shaunti didn't need a pep talk, and she didn't need my stellar business advice about how to approach CNN in a new way. All those things had already occurred to her. What she needed most was for me to share in her disappointment. For example, giving her a big hug and saying, "I'm so sorry. I know you were excited about being on CNN, and you must be really disappointed."

Since filtering out the problem and focusing on the feelings feels weird at first, it can be really easy to slip back into "man mode" and listen the old way, which may result in a bad back. From sleeping on the sofa. I'm just saying.

To save you the Sofa Step, here are a few hard-learned keys to success.

Key to Success 1: When She Wants to Talk, Give Her Your Full Attention

Most of us think, *I can listen well even if I'm doing something else.* Well, you probably can, if she is telling you that the car is making a funny noise. But feelings are a whole different landscape from fan belts. And it's *highly* unlikely that you will be one of the tiny percent of men who can truly grasp, acknowledge, and affirm those feelings while also watching Bear Grylls demonstrate how to skin a rattlesnake.

It makes a great difference when you take your attention *off* every other distraction and put it *on* her. It may also mean running interference when other distractions threaten.

For example, a year later, Shaunti still remembers a simple action I did when she really needed to talk and the kids kept interrupting. I asked the kids to play elsewhere for a minute, pulled her into the living room, sat down with her on the sofa, and asked her to share what was on her mind. Those two or three minutes were an incredibly good investment if they still make her feel loved a year later! And I have to confess that I have absolutely no memory of this event. Not because I do this all the time, but because it took so little time or effort!

Key to Success 2: Acknowledge Her Feelings Out Loud

Remember, she has absolutely no idea whether you understand her feelings unless you *show* it. Acknowledging to her what you're hearing—a simple verbal restatement of her words—is the magic bullet.

Thus, when I say to Shaunti, "I'm so sorry to hear that CNN didn't come through—that must have been so disappointing," she *feels* heard.

Key to Success 3: Affirm and Sympathize

No matter how good you are at acknowledging her feelings, all your brownie points go away if you then say, "But you shouldn't feel that way." Whether or not you think she *should* feel that way, it is vital to realize that she *does*. If acknowledging her feelings comes out as "I'm sorry you felt disappointed," then affirming them means recognizing (and maybe even saying) that it's okay that she felt disappointed.

Listening

> Affirming her feelings means recognizing (and maybe even saying) that it's okay that she felt disappointed.

If you don't honestly believe that, at least avoid trying to talk her out of feeling that way. The time will come later for philosophical discussions. Right now she needs the most important person in her life to try to share her feelings and, as the Bible puts it, "Rejoice with those who rejoice, weep with those who weep." As two women told us:

- "Trying to talk me out of my feelings doesn't accomplish what he's trying to accomplish. In fact, it makes me feel absolutely terrible, like my husband doesn't care one jot about how I feel."

- "Men don't realize the value of affirming our feelings when they seem irrational or out of proportion to them. If a man could just grasp the value of that, he could cut arguments or long discussion times in half."

Key to Success 4: Realize That She's Probably Not Attacking You

I can't emphasize enough how important this is. When emotions start flying around, especially if the conversation is about our relationship, I can so quickly conclude that Shaunti is attacking *me*. If she feels unhappy, I—like most men—assume she thinks I blew it.

But I'm realizing that often a man's performance isn't even

on his wife's mind. Instead, her brain wiring means she best processes thoughts and feelings by talking about them. And the *only*
way she can do that with us is if we don't get defensive and take it
personally. Consider what one survey taker said she most wished
her husband knew:

> That when I tell him how I feel inside about something
> concerning our relationship—that I am just trying to
> share my feeling with him so we can discuss it. He takes
> it as criticism and turns it around so I feel like the bad
> guy for bringing it up. He says, "I never do anything
> right," or "I can never please you," which isn't true. And
> so the problem never really gets discussed. I wish he
> could understand that it's important for me to be able to
> talk about these things and understand that I'm not just
> being critical.

Key to Success 5: Help Her Understand Your Limits in Advance

Because most women don't have an emotional or even physical
limit to their ability to listen and process emotion, they don't
understand that most men do. I can be totally *willing* to listen
to Shaunti share her feelings about something. But just like my
body would shut down if I tried to run too many miles, my

brain starts to check out after a while, whether I want it to or not.

So set yourself up for success by mentioning this to your wife or girlfriend at some neutral time, and help her to understand the limits of *your* particular listening capacity.

Be reassured, though, that listening won't usually mean a marathon. As one male marriage counselor told us, "Guys need to know that their wives aren't looking to them to be their best girlfriend and listen for hours. For most women, even taking a fifteen-minute walk with them a few evenings a week would totally fill their need."

If we get the listening sequence right—addressing her feelings first—then the right and healing solutions will follow.

Step 2: Offer Solutions Together

You'll remember that most of the women in the survey found suggestions to be a negative if their husbands weren't listening and being emotionally supportive first. But next we asked, when the women set aside how they felt about their man's emotional support, how would they feel about his actual suggestions? Thankfully, more than two-thirds said they were helpful suggestions—and we can infer that more than 80 percent actually *agreed* with the suggested solution! Just 19 percent said that the solution itself would not be a good one.

Consider times when you have actually been in the type of situation described in the previous question. Setting aside how you feel about your husband/significant other's emotional support, how useful or valuable are his actual suggestions? (Choose one answer.)

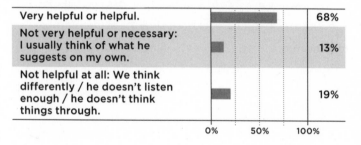

Very helpful or helpful.	68%
Not very helpful or necessary: I usually think of what he suggests on my own.	13%
Not helpful at all: We think differently / he doesn't listen enough / he doesn't think things through.	19%

WITH GREAT POWER

When I was a kid, one of my favorite Marvel Comics characters was Spider-Man—the average guy who has great power thrust upon him and has to learn how to use it well. He is challenged with one of my favorite quotes of all time: "With great power comes great responsibility."

Which brings us to more good news for guys on listening.

Virtually all the data in this chapter point to one often-overlooked principle for a man who wants a happy relationship: *the person who listens well holds enormous power.* If we can learn to

Listening

listen the way our mate needs us to, we have great power to defuse conflicting emotions, power to acknowledge and affirm—and, yes, power to *then* help find solutions.

Most of all, though, when you and I listen, we wield great power to tell the woman we care about most that she is truly loved. As one woman told us, "After a great conversation, I just want to kiss him and tell him how very, very much I appreciate him."

7

WITH SEX, HER "NO" DOESN'T MEAN YOU

*How her desires are impacted
by her unique wiring and
why your ego shouldn't be*

> *Physically, women tend to crave sex less often than
> men do—and it is usually not related to your
> desirability.*

his chapter will be the ultimate test of your manhood. I'm
going to ask you to do two things, and do them at the same
time:

1. Think clearly.
2. About sex.

Sex

I've noticed, and probably so have you, that what we men do so well as separate tasks—clear thinking and sex—we routinely, embarrassingly, miserably fail at doing together.

As I found out after I got a full dose of the honest truth from about 450 women in Colorado.

There I was, the only guy, listening while Shaunti presented what she'd learned about men while writing *For Women Only*. It was a weird and wonderful experience.

And here was the wonderful part—at least at first. During a lively question-and-answer session, almost all the questions focused on sex! I was so amazed at the ladies' one-track minds that I could barely listen to the questions. I knew that my buddies back in Atlanta would be as ecstatic as I was at the idea that women really did want sex more than we'd thought.

Fast-forward to Jeff and Shaunti doing in-depth focus groups of women for this book. I am over the weirdness by now, but unfortunately the wonderful is no longer in sight. Instead, what I'm hearing doesn't jibe at all with the good news I'd heard in the Rockies. Finally, I do my best to describe for these women the absolute obsession with sex among their counterparts at higher elevations.

The women stare at me politely. Then one breaks the news. "Well, um, since Shaunti's book emphasized how central sex is to a man's emotional well-being, the women were probably wondering how to handle their man's requests."

Okay, I think to myself. *Cool. Nothing wrong with that.*

She sees that clear thinking has yet to occur. "And it was *not* because they want sex so much," she continues. "A lot of women don't have that same need to *pursue* sex as much as guys do. So they were simply trying to figure out what on earth to do!"

In desperation I shoot a questioning look at my wife, but Shaunti is already nodding. "I'm afraid so," she says. "That's exactly what was happening."

THE WHOPPING BIG MISS

How could I—a smart, married, and extremely likable man— have completely missed a full dose of the honest truth about sex from 450 women? And I hadn't just missed it. What I thought I heard was almost the direct opposite of what they were actually saying.

After spending hours going over surveys and listening to focus groups, I've come to believe that my whopping big miss is pretty much what men do in their marriages every day. We think male and female humans are the same creatures, only with different and nicely matching body parts. We assume we have the same sexual wiring. So when there seems to be a mismatch, we have no idea why. As one of my puzzled buddies put it, "If sex is free and it's fun, why does she not want *lots* of free fun?"

Now, we do know that in some marriages it's the woman

who is pining for more—one in four, according to our survey. So if you're in that situation, you're not alone.

Of course some wives indicated that they and their husbands were happily on the same page—to the envy of all. But since we have limited space, we're focusing on the apparent majority of husbands who want "more and better" and don't know what to do about it.[3]

> ◁ "If sex is free and it's fun, why does she not want lots of free fun?"

Thankfully, solutions exist, and our research confirms good news for men who find themselves in that situation. In particular: most women do care about what their man wants. And they *do* care about sex. And they *do* want great sexual relationships with their husbands.

But to get there, we need to do that "thinking clearly" thing.

THE IMPOSSIBLE SURPRISE ABOUT THE SEX GAP: "IT'S NOT YOU"

If you're a typical married male, you probably want more sex with your wife than you get. But that's not the end of the story. I know, because in Shaunti's professional survey for *For Women*

Only, 97 percent of men said "getting enough sex" wasn't, by it-self, enough—they wanted to feel genuinely wanted.

Men are powerfully driven by the emotional need to feel *desired* by our wives, and we filter everything through that grid. *Do I feel desired or not desired by my wife?* If we feel our wives truly want us sexually, we feel confident, powerful, alive, and loved. If we don't, we feel depressed, angry, and alone. And this goes way beyond the amount of sex we're having.

But here's where the first breakdown in communication comes between the average husband and wife. Our surveys showed a startling, hard-to-believe, but oddly encouraging truth for men. *While you want to be genuinely desired by your wife, her lower level of desire for sex likely has nothing to do with your desirability.*

You might want to read that again. And if you think about it, that's actually good news for the 99.9 percent of us who don't look like a shirtless Matthew McConaughey.

Here are the facts. Among survey takers who wanted less sex than their husbands, fully 75 percent indicated that it had *nothing* to do with his desirability, sexual prowess, or general studliness. In fact, of the remaining 25 percent, less than 4 percent said their lower interest in sex was specifically because their husband was "not attractive or desirable." (The hesitation of the other 21 per-cent primarily had to do with not anticipating pleasure, including for physical reasons.)

Sex

One survey taker spoke for that astounding 96 percent of women when she said that the one thing she most wished her husband knew was "that just because I do not want sex as often as he does, I still love him deeply and find him very attractive."

> While you want to be genuinely desired by your wife, her lower level of desire for sex likely has nothing to do with your desirability.

Look at the top three reasons (by a wide margin) that women gave for wanting less sex:

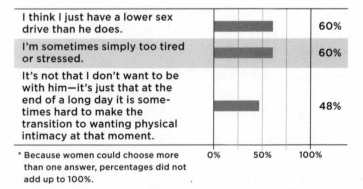

Among women who said they wanted less sex than their husbands, the top three reasons why:*

I think I just have a lower sex drive than he does.		60%
I'm sometimes simply too tired or stressed.		60%
It's not that I don't want to be with him—it's just that at the end of a long day it is sometimes hard to make the transition to wanting physical intimacy at that moment.		48%

* Because women could choose more than one answer, percentages did not add up to 100%.

0%   50%   100%

Our results show that, although there certainly are issues that can be addressed, the frequency gap is usually *not* because a wife doesn't desire her husband. In fact, usually, she does! Instead, in the great majority of cases where there is a frequency gap, the cliché is actually true: "Look, it's not you. It's me."

> The frequency gap is usually not because a wife doesn't desire her husband.

If you're still thinking clearly, your brain likely has ground to a halt on an apparent impossibility: *I can't imagine finding my wife attractive, being in love with her, and not wanting to have sex with her often! So how can she be that way?*

But remember, that's guy thinking, and we're trying to learn female thinking. For the moment, take a step away from that seeming impossibility and let your driving question instead be, *So if it's not about me, what is it about?*

"SO IF IT'S NOT ABOUT ME...?" FIVE TRUTHS ABOUT WOMEN AND SEX

Shaunti and I want to relay what women around the country told us about their sexual wiring and what they want to give—and get—from their man. These five revelations, should you choose to believe them, have the potential to radically improve this area of your marriage.

Truth 1: She Has a Lower Sex Drive than You, and She'd Change That Fact If She Could

Physiological Fact 1: Brain scientists explain that the average woman simply has less testosterone and other sexually assertive hormones than the average man and therefore has less of an urge to *pursue* sex. This doesn't mean she doesn't want it or won't enjoy it once it's happening, but seeking it out isn't usually on her mind.

> This doesn't mean she doesn't want it or won't enjoy it once it's happening, but seeking it out isn't usually on her mind.

Most men know this fact, but—Physiological Fact 2—we forget it on a regular basis. Like, every evening. We forget because we can't really feel the truth of it, especially when she says or implies "no" the minute we show sexual interest. Admit it: an analysis of physiological differences is not where your mind goes following another nonencounter. So let's step back and look at some implications of her physiology:

> ▶ *Lower level of sexually assertive hormones = less craving for sex*

Not *no* craving, mind you, just *less*. It's a fact, and we need to stop assuming it has something to do with *us*.

As several experts explained, this is a complex issue, but it boils down to the surprising fact that there are actually two different types of sexual desire: assertive desire and receptive desire. Where men have more testosterone-type hormones linked to assertive desire, women have more estrogen, which is tied to receptive desire. This means that they tend to be *available* but simply don't have as much craving to pursue it.[4] And studies have shown that a common form of birth control (the Pill) can reduce libido even further. It doesn't help that movies, television shows, and advertisements seem to imply that all women would be sexually charged bimbo wannabes if you were just enough of a stud.

On the survey, when we asked women what they most wished their husbands understood, one wife put it this way: "I want him to know I don't love him less just because my sex drive isn't as strong as his."

▶ *Lower level of sexually assertive hormones = less likely to initiate sex*

As one book put it, "Receptive doesn't necessarily mean passive [but] available, and perhaps willing, but without the initiative to pursue sex."[5] Related to this, we received a telling e-mail from a man whose wife had read Shaunti's book *For Women Only*.

Sex

My wife then explained to me that she simply has no physical drive to pursue sex. When we are having sex, she says that she loves it. The problem is that otherwise, sex just never occurs to her, whereas there is never a time when it does *not* occur to me! Thankfully, after reading *For Women Only,* my wife understood how important sex really is to me and has even begun to initiate sex. She does it because she wants to show that she loves me. It works…

In one of our focus groups, a woman said,

I just don't feel that drive to go after physical pleasure as often. For me, it's about once every ten days that *I'm* the one looking for the physical pleasure. The other times are because he needs it. And from my standpoint, it's time to be together, it's uninterrupted time, it's a way to have his undivided attention. Not that it's not physically great once we get started—it is! It's just that for me, there's usually not the drive to start.

▶ *Lower level of sexually assertive hormones = more susceptibility to nonsexual distractions*

Like a noise from the kid's room. Like a headache. Like stress or leftover thoughts from her day. Like exhaustion.

She's not making it up. In relation to her lower sex drive, she's more sensitive to hindrances and feels them more intensely than you or I would. As one woman said, "For guys, it seems, sex provides relief or escape from exhaustion. For women, we have to pull ourselves out of exhaustion in order to want to have sex."

> She's more sensitive to hindrances and feels them more intensely than you or I would.

But there's reassuring news too. Not only is the woman in your life not making up the hindrances to sex she experiences, *she would readily change her sexual responsiveness if she could.* Look at the data:

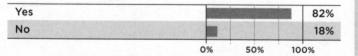

(Answered by women who said they wanted less sex than their husbands.) If you could magically change your sex drive and/or some of the reasons you don't want sex as much as your husband does, would you? (Choose one answer.)

Yes	82%
No	18%

0%   50%   100%

Sex

You can see that more than eight out of ten wives would prefer to want sex as much as their husbands...if they could. (And among happily married women, that desire was almost 100 percent.)

Truth 2: She Needs More Warmup Time than You

A guy's sexual motor is pretty much always running. Pop the clutch and go. Not so for a woman. But once her sexual motor is warmed up and running, she is raring to go, just like we are. One respondent told us:

> I wish my husband would understand that as much as I love to be intimate with him, there are times when it takes a long time to "get me there." I have been busy running after kids all day, cleaning, cooking, etc. Sex also helps me to unwind, but I need a little help. He seems to think that just because he is ready and set, I should be too. He gets frustrated because I do not seem like I am enjoying him, but if he would just take his time, we would both enjoy the experience more.

Another woman provided a great word picture:

> It's not that I don't *want* to make love, but at the end of a long day with four kids, my mind is set on a course like a cruise ship headed for port…port being that quiet bit of space a mom anticipates when the kids are asleep, the chores done, and the house quiet. And just as I'm within

sight of that port, my hubby rolls over and says, "Whatcha doing over there?" It's not that I don't want to be with him, but mentally, it's like trying to stop a cruise ship that's going full steam ahead and making it turn on a dime. I can't quite turn off the day and do an about-face in the blink of an eye like he can.

Many other women echoed what one said she most wished her husband knew: "How much I truly and deeply love him, but my body just doesn't have the same sexual drive as his *until we are engaged in the act* [emphasis added]. Then I'm *very* into it."

The "very into it" part is great news. But to get there, what this means in practice is one of two things: either (1) she needs you to take it slow, to give her brain a chance to catch up, or even better, (2) she needs what we call anticipation time.

> Either she needs you to take it slow, or she needs anticipation time.

Look at the anticipation example one woman shared:

My husband and I don't get too many nights alone, but we carved out a dinner date one night, and while we were having dinner he whispered in my ear, "I can't wait to get

Sex

home and have my dessert." I knew the dessert was
me, and I don't think I've ever eaten so fast in my life.
I couldn't wait to get home.

I know we guys think that if we were desirable enough, sex
would be spontaneous because our wife couldn't keep her hands
off us. No such luck. If she's like most women and wired for receptive desire, even with the wonderful dinner date you planned,
the flowers you brought home, or your thoughtfulness in washing
the dishes so she could get to bed earlier—all that by itself doesn't
mean she's thinking about sex.

Don't despair, though. The key is working with her wiring
rather than wishing it were different, and we get to that in the
ultra-important "what do we do about it" section coming up.

Truth 3: Your Body (No Matter How Much of a Stud You Are) Does Not by Itself Turn on Her Body

Maybe you should sit down. Take a breath. Clear that head. Because average male assumptions simply will *not* work here.

Let's start with how *you* work. Your eyes see an attractive
woman, and generally your body registers attraction. Instantly. If
the attractive woman isn't wearing much, your physical reaction
is even stronger. It's like metal shavings pulled toward a magnet.

Your wife, though, is not like you. She is not sexually aroused simply by seeing you at your studly best. If you are looking particularly handsome or sexy, she *will* notice and she *will* find you attractive. But—get this—her body is still not lusting over your body. Listen in on an actual conversation relayed to us by one long-married couple:

SHE (delivering the shocking news): "There isn't one thing about your body that makes me sexually attracted to you and want to go to bed with you."

HE (disbelieving): "I thought I was sexy and good looking. You always told me I was!"

SHE (calmly): "You are. But that has nothing to do with why I want to have sex with you. (Noticing his blank look, she continues.) Really. Nothing about your naked body makes me hot—that is, until *after* we're sexually involved."

HE (sputtering): "But...I...how...?"

SHE (reassuring): "Babe, I like you and I like your naked body. It's sweet, actually, and you're mine. But it's not like my body is lusting after yours."

HE (grasping): "What...what about me in my black leather jacket? You always come up to me and growl. Are you saying...?"

Sex

SHE: "Nope, even you in that jacket. You look totally hot,
mind you, and I do want to be with you. But I'm just
telling you, physically my body does not become
sexually aroused *one bit*!"

The truth is that our wives can find us desirable and attractive but still not be turned on by that alone. Women get turned
on in other, less visible but equally powerful ways. And that leads
to another truth about sex that most guys have heard over and
over…but have never quite come to terms with.

Truth 4: For Her, Sex Starts in Her Heart

Her body's ability to respond to you sexually is tied to how she
feels *emotionally* about you at the moment. If she's not feeling
anything in her heart, her body's sex switches are all the way over
on Off. Even if you put on your black leather jacket.

> For her, what's in her heart about you
> and how she can respond sexually meld
> into one.

One consequence: where you might greatly desire her even
though she was rude to you this morning, how *you* treated *her*
this morning really matters. She's not keeping score, by the way.

She just can't help it. For her, those two things—what's in her heart about you and how she can respond sexually—meld into one.

One woman explained it to her husband this way: "All my power to turn you on is how I look. But where *you* have power, and where I don't, is how you treated me today. It's all emotional."

We talked a lot about your wife's need for closeness and affirmation—how to treat her today—in chapters 2 and 4. Bet you didn't realize we were talking about sex too!

Of course, there's a reverse consequence of her "start in the heart" need: the potential for hurt feelings. Shaunti's honest thought here is that if a relationship has become strained and a wife says, "The only time you're interested in me is for sex," realize that by definition, she's feeling neglected and perhaps even used.

Now, you may be initiating sex in order to try to make it better and get those feelings of closeness back, but women aren't wired that way. If they are feeling serious emotional distance or hurt, sex does not fix it—and it may exacerbate it.

Truth 5: She Wants Pleasure as Much as You Do, but If It's Not Happening, She May Be Reluctant

Okay. This might be difficult, but face it we must: some wives don't experience pleasure when they are intimate with their

Sex

husbands. According to our survey, this is an issue for only a relatively small minority—just 16 percent said that was why they desired less sex. But that means it is still an issue in one out of every six or seven marriages. And only if we are willing to bring up this subject with our wife, set aside our defenses, and hear what she has to say are we going to learn if this has been a reason for her lack of interest. One woman wrote to Shaunti,

> Men think women aren't as interested in sex as they are.
> But some men need to know that their wives are just not
> experiencing sexual satisfaction. Although they might be
> enjoying the process, they may not be 'finishing' it. This
> is a difficult subject, and many women don't want to talk
> about it because they don't want to depress their husband
> or make him feel inadequate. So they protect his feelings
> at the expense of their own. But if a woman isn't crossing
> the finish line, running the race just isn't going to be as
> important to her—which only makes it easier to find
> excuses to sit it out.

I suppose you and I only have to think about what it would be like if we always "went there" sexually only to never "get there" to know how frustrating and demotivating that would be.

Clearly, it's time for you and me to sweep up our rattled egos, maybe throw on our black leather jacket just for luck, and go looking for answers.

A GUIDE FOR ORDINARY HUSBANDS

When one of my friends heard that we were writing this chapter, he chuckled. "If you can get the average husband sex even a dozen more times a year, men will build statues to you in city parks across the country."

So the following is my stab at immortality.

Think of these practical suggestions as directions on a map—directions that apply those little-understood truths we talked about and get the two of you where you both want to be.

> "If you can get the average husband sex even a dozen more times a year, men will build statues to you in city parks across the country."

1. Pay Attention to Her Outside the Bedroom and Help Her Out—it's the Little Things

Great sex starts with helping your wife feel happy and close to you outside the bedroom. On the survey we asked each woman who wanted less or the same amount of sex what their husband could

Sex

do to increase the chances that they would want to make love more frequently. Look at the top three responses:

Are there things that your husband can do to increase the chances that you will want to make love more frequently? Please rate the helpfulness of each of the following statements: (Choose one answer for each statement.)

	NOT PARTICULARLY HELPFUL	VERY HELPFUL
Maintain or increase his level of emotional attention to me	27%	73%
Create a context where he often shows me little gestures of love throughout the day	29%	71%
Engage in caring listening and conversation regularly	33%	67%

Those helpful things that build closeness are the little things we've mentioned throughout the book, such as:

- putting your hand on the small of her back to guide her through a parking lot.
- reassuring her of your love when you two are at odds.
- getting up from the dinner table to get the fire starter so she can "close the window" and enjoy dinner.
- listening for her feelings and saying, "I'm so sorry you were disappointed, honey."

And it's not just emotional attention that matters. On the survey, up to 70 percent of women said that simple helpfulness around the house would increase their interest—if only because they would have more energy! (The highest agreement came among moms with school-age kids.) A study by famed marriage psychologist John Gottman confirmed that men who do more housework have both happier marriages *and* better sex lives.[6]

> Great sex starts with helping your wife feel happy and close to you outside the bedroom.

As one stay-at-home mom said, "My husband and I have a little joke between us. I say, 'Honey, there is nothing more sexy than watching you clean something. And there's *really* nothing more sexy than watching you clean the toilet!' It's all about feeling that he wants to take care of me."

2. Give Chase, Agent 007. The Time for Pursuit Is...Always

I love this comment that came in to Shaunti's website:

A woman needs to feel sexy to her man. But many men do not spend the time or effort in affirming their spouse sexually *outside* of the bedroom. That means, when we're in the bedroom, it's difficult for the woman to figure out whether he really wants her or whether he's just trying to satisfy his own need. A woman who knows she is sexy to her husband outside the bedroom will never have an excuse at lovemaking time!

Another married woman told us:

Women want to be romantically pursued. It's as powerful as the man's sex drive. Men think women can't resist James Bond because of his body, his money, or his fast cars. But that stuff is almost irrelevant. James Bond is *romantic.* He pursues a woman, flirts with her, woos her. I think women are a lot more aware of the need to work hard at meeting their man's sex-drive needs than men are aware of the need to work at meeting her romantic-pursuit needs. Guys have to realize that for a woman, they go hand in hand!

> "Women want to be romantically pursued. It's as powerful as the man's sex drive."

Whether it's calls, notes, conversations, or simply admiring eye contact, the whole point of pursuit to a woman is that you notice her, you're interested in her, and you belong to her...and she belongs to *you*. Remember chapter 2? There will never be a day when she permanently feels loved. She needs to feel, day to day, that you are choosing her all over again.

Of course, it won't help you at all if your wife feels she's only being pursued *so that* you can get sex! In the busyness of life, we guys sometimes simply forget about doing the loving little things just because we love our wives, so the thought of sex becomes a sort of trigger to remember to be a bit more attentive. But that means we risk training our wives to be cynical and to suspect total self-interest on our part whenever they see our attentive gestures—it looks like we only care about them when we want sex! So there's a need for a little reconditioning. Sometimes we need to hug her just to hug her. Send her a sweet e-mail during the day, rub her back, help her out around the house, cuddle with her in bed...and not ask for sex. At least sometimes.

3. Give Her Anticipation Time

This step is the one most guys miss, yet it may be the most important. We need to think about ways to get her anticipation engine running several hours in advance. That's because you can do everything else we're saying—be kind and thoughtful, share chores around the house, and be the best listener on the planet—but if she has receptive desire, she's *still* not likely to be thinking about

Sex

sex. So find ways to let her know what you'd love to happen later…and give her time to savor what you have in mind.

One woman showed how simple that can be. "One thing that will help get a wife in the mood is something as small as a flirting call or e-mail. Something like 'I saw you getting dressed this morning and I can't stop thinking about you. I can't wait to see you undress tonight.'"

That's an easy chip shot if I ever saw one.

> "One thing that will help get a wife in the mood is something as small as a flirting call or e-mail."

Another woman proposed something that other women agreed might be helpful, as nonspontaneous as it sounds to men:

With kids and jobs, for me, sex needs to be planned and expected or it just won't happen. He thinks having set days to expect it means that it is just another thing to check off my to-do list. But actually, when I have it in mind to expect it, then it is really a reward at the end of a long day. If I don't know to expect it, then that *is* when it becomes a chore and just another thing that needs to get done. The planning means I am making him a priority, not putting him on a list.

4. When in Doubt, Ask Her

Just like the existence of this whole chapter, this particular to-do runs against the grain of my middle-class, midwestern, don't-talk-about-sex reticence. While it may not be comfortable, you just need to ask your wife what she likes, what she doesn't, and how to improve. If there is an issue, it could be as simple as personal hygiene. (Several women, upon finding out that we were writing this chapter, asked Shaunti privately, "You will tell them to brush their teeth, won't you?") And make sure she knows that you *want* to know whether she's not only enjoying the race but also crossing the finish line.

If the two of you aren't clicking in this area, it's also possible other things could be going on. I'm not an expert, but if your wife seems to love you but avoids sex (or finds it emotionally painful), make sure there aren't any deep-seated issues that need addressing. If there are, be her advocate in getting the help she needs to address them.

And I know we guys pretend it's never an issue, but if by chance *you're* the one experiencing "performance" problems, be brave and seek help from your doctor or counselor. One woman wrote about this, "His unwillingness to seek medical help is breaking my heart."

You have a lot of life ahead, and your wife wants to enjoy it with you. One wife put it well:

Sex

I appreciate feeling like we are team players, not just in the bedroom, but in everything. After a long day, I want to feel supported and uplifted, just as he does. And of course, theoretically, a good roll in the hay will do that! But there are times at the end of the day when I feel as if I can't quite get started. I want him to be sensitive to me and minister to me! He is who I am counting on for this. And I know if I can, he'll be able to count on me too.

8

THE GIRL IN THE MIRROR

What the little girl inside your woman is dying to hear from you— and how to guard your answer well

> *Inside your smart, secure wife lives a little girl who deeply needs to know that you find her beautiful— and that you only have eyes for her.*

When we were writing the original edition of this book, our daughter was five years old and definitely at that "Daddy's girl" stage. She could whack a pretty good line drive for her age. But she was happiest, I think, when she was dancing for me in a consignment-store costume dress Shaunti had bought for her. It was pink and had a twirly skirt. Pink and twirly matters a lot when you're five. I can still see her twirling around our living room. Absolutely beaming with delight. Twirl left. Pause. Twirl right.

"Daddy, watch!" she calls as she spins and the skirt does its thing. "Daddy, look at me! Do you think I'm pretty?"

If you've ever had a little girl twirling around your house, you know what I was thinking right then: *Lord, just let me hold on to this moment! Please don't let my little girl grow up.*

That's what this chapter is about. Because you see, in a way, little girls never really do.

THE GIRL INSIDE

Would it surprise you to know that your gifted, hardworking, secure, grown-up wife is still (silently) asking the same question, *Do you think I'm pretty?* Only now it's *you* watching. It's you she's asking, you who will decide her haunting question, *Am I beautiful?* And even more important: *Am I beautiful...to you?*

Am I beautiful...to you?

In a culture where women are bombarded with expectations to lose weight, look younger, look sexy—actually, look perfect— that question has killer consequences. It also gives clued-in men an opportunity that we didn't even know we had to affirm our wives in a very important way.

On our survey most women told us they had a "deep need or desire" to know that their husbands or boyfriends found them beautiful. And younger women were even more likely to have that need. Among women age forty-five and younger, more than three out of four felt this need (77 percent). With women thirty-five and younger the percentage rose to 84 percent.

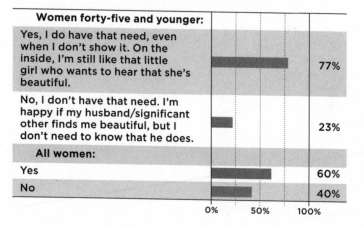

Regardless of how you think you look, do you have a deep need or desire to know that your husband/significant other finds you beautiful? Which answer most closely describes you? (Choose one answer.)

Women forty-five and younger:		
Yes, I do have that need, even when I don't show it. On the inside, I'm still like that little girl who wants to hear that she's beautiful.		77%
No, I don't have that need. I'm happy if my husband/significant other finds me beautiful, but I don't need to know that he does.		23%
All women:		
Yes		60%
No		40%

0%   50%   100%

Women with children at home were also much more likely to have a deep desire to hear that their husbands found them beautiful—up to 85 percent of them. One survey taker said the thing

Beauty

she most wished her husband understood was that "women need to be reassured often that they are beautiful and they are loved."

The good news is that when their men *do* tell them they're beautiful, the consequences are…beautiful! Almost 90 percent said it made them feel good or made their day. And that percentage was still huge (77 percent) even among the mostly older women who said they didn't *need* to hear it! Only a tiny number (3 percent) said it made no difference.

How beneficial is it to you when your husband/significant other tells you that he finds you beautiful? (Choose one answer.)

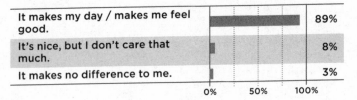

It makes my day / makes me feel good.	89%
It's nice, but I don't care that much.	8%
It makes no difference to me.	3%

0%   50%   100%

ONE GUY, ONE MIRROR, ONE HAMMER

You might be thinking what Shaunti has already heard from a few skeptical women: *Why is this chapter focusing so much on a woman's looks? Shouldn't we as a society be getting past that?*

Well, here's the thing: This *isn't* really about a woman's looks.

It *is* about what a woman feels about herself and the fact that her man has a great ability to build her up or tear her down in that area.

"Wait a minute!" I can hear you saying. "But she *knows* I think she's beautiful."

Does she? Have you told her recently? More recently than that time last year when you two got all dressed up for that wedding? You *did* tell her she looked beautiful then, didn't you? Sure you did.

Okay, you *probably* did.

I too think my wife is beautiful, but until Shaunti and I talked about this chapter, I realized that I rarely tell her so. It just wasn't something I thought she needed to hear or that I needed to do.

Then we talked. Oh, boy. All has *not* been well in the land of the free and the home of the Braves.

What I've since learned, and what kept surprising me on our surveys, is that even if a woman knows in her head that her husband finds her beautiful, *she still needs to hear it.* And often. Every day is good.

She still needs to hear it:

- no matter how successful, self-assured, or mature she is.
- no matter how long you've been together.
- no matter how gorgeous other people might tell her she is.
- no matter how moved to tears of gratitude you were last time you said it.
- no matter how old or young she is.

> Even if a woman knows in her head that her husband finds her beautiful, she still needs to *hear* it.

As it turns out, your wife's continuing desire to feel beautiful—and to be beautiful *for you*—is a deeply rooted need that explains a lot of other behaviors that have baffled men for centuries. For example, have you ever wondered:

- why, after trying on outfit after outfit, she gets frustrated and declares that she has nothing to wear?
- why she wants to buy new clothes even if she knows you are on a tight budget or even if few of her clothes could possibly be considered old?
- why she's always asking you how she looks when there are mirrors in the bedroom and the bathroom?
- why she asks, "Do these pants make me look fat?" when what she really means is, "Tell me I'm not fat"?
- why it's such a big deal if your eyes linger on another beautiful woman?

Listen, after an inexcusably long learning curve, I've come to realize a few crucial facts about beauty and my wife. These facts are fundamental in every marriage and have the power to radically change your relationship and mine for the better, beginning with the next words we speak to her.

Fact 1. That little dancing girl is still very much alive inside my dear wife. Only now she twirls for me.

Fact 2. In our marriage, whether I find her beautiful may or may not be foremost in my mind, but it is an everyday (even if subconscious) issue for her.

Fact 3. In our house, there's really only one mirror. And that mirror is me.

Fact 4. Every day I can reflect back to her the words she so needs to hear. But if I don't, I leave her vulnerable to both her inner questions and external pressure from an intimidating world.

Fact 5. In my hand I hold a hammer.

I hope you're beginning to see why a clued-in husband or boyfriend can create so much good, and why a clueless one can cause so much damage.

And I haven't even told you what the hammer is yet.

> Every day I can reflect back to her the words she so needs to hear.

THE UGLY TRUTH ABOUT FEMALE BEAUTY IN OUR WORLD

Just so you and I know that our wives or girlfriends aren't the only body obsessed or oversensitive women around, let's hear what some

Beauty

women told us about the pressure they feel from our culture and from themselves. It's almost like they must fight their way through a war zone every day—and men don't even realize it. Listen in:

- "I know in my head that I am not unattractive. I wouldn't wear a bikini anymore, but people still tell me I'm pretty or that I look really slim in that outfit or whatever. But in my heart, I don't believe it. Because my head is also very aware of all my flaws, especially since the kids came along. Almost every time I see a picture of myself, I cringe inside. I'm guessing that my husband thinks I'm attractive, but I can't think of the last time he made it a point to tell me so. If he would, it sure would counter that secret negativity about myself that I feel inside."

- "Every day we are bombarded with these images all around us of how we are supposed to look. We have this fear that we feel like we'll always have to live up to our husband's expectation of this perfect Holly-wood body image, and we know we can't do that. Somehow we get this idea that if we don't, oh, no, maybe his attention will turn elsewhere. It's a very insecure feeling, even if it's totally ridiculous. We may know in our heads that that's not true, but that head knowledge doesn't do anything to counter our silent insecurity."

And last, here's one that may be hard for any father or married man to hear:

- "In this culture, women are not being protected emotionally. They are being humiliated."

Do you really think it's possible for you and me to understand just how on stage and under review our wife or girlfriend feels every day? I have to admit—until now I haven't given much thought to how demeaning and threatening our world is for Shaunti and other women. Or how demeaning their own thoughts about themselves can be, even if they hide them well.

When I think back on typical male responses to this unseen struggle, I'm not encouraged. For Shaunti, I'm the one man in her life who can really relieve the pressure and make her feel beautiful. But because I haven't known I've needed to, my response on an average day to her unseen need has tended to be...a yawn. Or even irritation at how long she's taking to get dressed.

Or on a good day, maybe, "You look nice."

> I'm the one man in her life who can really relieve the pressure and make her feel beautiful.

Guys, we are divinely positioned to encourage and build up the woman we love. We can't be nodding off in the living room chair while the little girl twirls in front of us.

So now that we're awake to the problem, what can we do?

REFLECT BACK
THE TRUTH ABOUT HER

Remember, you're not just the guy who shares her space, you're her most important mirror—the man who can reflect back to her how lovely you think she is. The man whose opinions of her are the best antidote for the damaging internal dialogue and external pressure that stalk her thoughts. So how should and could you respond for the greatest benefit to her—and you?

> You're not just the guy who shares her space, you're her most important mirror.

Say It

Just think of a few affirming words—"You look beautiful today" (or your own version)—and *say* them. That kind of compliment might not feel natural to you at first, but if you stick with it, it can eventually feel as familiar as "Pass the remote."

Whenever possible, your guy-mirror talk should be specific. "A lot of women are so desperate for specific, honest compliments," one wife told us. "We're dying of thirst for them. I think guys probably often think them but don't say them. But I hope they can learn to say them, because one compliment can carry me for a long way."

A key time to practice affirmation is when you've both noticed another attractive person. One woman told us, "To me, the confirmation I need is something like this: 'Yes, that other woman is cute, but you're beautiful, and *you're mine*.' Those words would be such a help to me in consciously tearing down the insecurity I carry around."

Say It Now

It is also important to train yourself to say it when she needs it. In other words, right away. Whenever you think it. Or if she's just gotten dressed up to go out, what she's looking for is the immediate, reflexive response that proves you've been wowed. But as this story from one couple we talked to shows, we men have to practice putting ourselves in that frame of mind lest we send the wrong message!

> Train yourself to say it when she needs it—right away.

HER: After I get ready to go out somewhere, there's sort of a thirty-second rule. If he hasn't noticed me in thirty seconds, I guess I don't look good enough for him. So, okay, we were going out last night. I take a lot of time getting ready and spiffy for him, and I think I look

Beauty

pretty hot. I come downstairs and he doesn't say anything. So instantly I'm a bit deflated. We walk out of the house and climb into the car, and as we're backing out of the driveway, he notices that the little metal insignia on the car hood is crooked. He stops the car and gets out to straighten it. He noticed that, but he didn't notice *me*?

HIM (laughing ruefully): Pray for me, Jeff!

Erase "Fine" from Your Response Options

"Fine" is not fine unless used in the sense, "She's so fine!" "Fine" is what you mumbled to Mom when she asked how school went.

The problem is, we misunderstand the real question. When the woman in our life asks "How do I look?" or "Is what I'm wearing okay?" we think she's wondering if she looks presentable. But that's not it at all. What she's looking for is reassurance that we think she is beautiful, stunning, and so-glad-she's-mine. And "fine" or "okay" are not even on the same planet as that.

Answer Her Real Question: "Do I Still Rock Your World?"

And that gives us the answer to how we handle that dreaded question, "Do these jeans make me look fat?"

Oh boy.

We all instinctively feel that there is *no* safe answer to this question. But in this case, she's not asking "Can I walk out the door in this?" Instead, she's feeling insecure about her body, about her beauty, and whether you still love and appreciate her. Most of the time, in fact, what she's asking is, "After twenty years of marriage and two kids, do I still rock your world?" If you answer *that* question well, you're good to go.

My advice? Say "Babe, you look gorgeous" and hold her hand all the way into the restaurant.

There will be times, of course, when your wife truly wants feedback. If that's the case, ask her *in advance* to help you know when she needs reassurance versus when she needs to know if an outfit looks good. An agreed-upon question or cue is all you need. For example, Shaunti has told me that if she says "Does this outfit work?" she really wants me to be candid, so she doesn't wear something that I don't think does her justice.

What If I Agree There's an Issue to Work On?

If your wife or girlfriend is struggling with a real issue (she's twenty-five pounds overweight) rather than being dissatisfied with something she can't healthfully change (she thinks her nose is too big), realize that she feels terrible about it already. Knowing you are disappointed makes it worse. On the other hand, *if* she's seriously talking about losing weight—and you think she's inviting your input—let her know you're on her side. A good sentence

Beauty

starter might be, "I love you no matter what. But if this bothers you, how can I help?" Then be willing to help. That might mean handling the soccer run so she can hit the gym or forgoing your nightly ice cream if it tempts her too much.

Whenever possible, make the effort with her. But whatever happens, keep on affirming her in those areas you *do* find beautiful, including her loveliness as a person.

Don't Take "No" for an Answer

By now, you might be thinking, *But I try to compliment my wife—and she always brushes it off.* It's pretty easy to give up, thinking she doesn't need affirmation or that there's no point in expending the energy if she's not going to believe it. But here's a pointer from Shaunti: take her reluctance as a sign that she needs the affirmation even more. Remember, her flaws loom large in her mind—even if you hardly notice them.

> Tell her—often—that you truly don't notice what she thinks of as flaws and that you find her beautiful.

For her, knowing that you find her lovely outside *and* inside will go a long way. We've all seen examples where an otherwise plain-looking woman became absolutely beautiful in our eyes because she had the "beauty of a gentle and quiet spirit," as the apostle Peter put it. If your wife is a lovely person but knows that her teeth are crooked or her post-childbearing stomach is no longer flat, tell her—often—that you truly don't notice what she thinks of as flaws. Tell her that her inner loveliness radiates through her, and that you and everyone else find her beautiful.

View Cost as an Investment

A lot of husbands struggle with their wives' desire to spend money on clothes, makeup, or beauty treatments. I hope by now you're seeing what's really happening here—she's trying to stay in the center of your field of vision and to bolster her own internal gauge of how she feels about herself.

No one is saying households should throw budget caution out the window. But what might appear a nonessential to us men might be a budget priority for her that she is willing to make trade-offs for. Here's a note Shaunti received on this topic:

> Please explain to the guys how important clothes are to women. Please try to explain how frumpy and unattractive we feel in old clothes, whether they are worn out or just out-of-date. A couple of my best friends struggle with this in their marriages; it's a common problem.

Now it's time to squarely address what may be the most important beauty connection of all. You and I can do an excellent

Beauty

job of reflecting our wife's beauty back to her and *still* cause enormous damage. How?

Fact 5: In my hand I hold a hammer.

THE HAMMER DROPS: LOOKING ELSEWHERE

We now know that women are powerfully affirmed by knowing that their husbands find them beautiful. But that power has a dark side. Because if a woman sees her husband's eyes *also* affirming the beauty of other women, she ceases to feel special. Suddenly, not only is she not affirmed, she's in competition with the world again—including for the attention of the one man she thought she already had. That's when the hammer hits the mirror that's you—the most important mirror in her life—and shatters it.

> If a woman sees her husband's eyes *also* affirming the beauty of other women, she ceases to feel special.

Now, because women are not as visually wired as we are, there are bound to be some misunderstandings here—some conflicts between what we consider innocent and what our women think. We may think, *My wife knows it's just a guy thing and I don't love this other woman I'm looking at.* Yes, sometimes it can simply be admiring beauty. And yes, God created a beautiful world—and populating it with attractive people is consistent with His artistry. But the challenge with looking at a beautiful woman is the speed at which admiration morphs into something else. Looking at the sweeping vista of the Rockies just doesn't run the risk of my next thought being *I wonder what those mountains would look like without all that snow on them.*

I urge you not to settle for what many in our culture consider acceptable compromises in this area. The New Testament sets a pretty high standard: "Do not conform any longer to the pattern of this world, but be transformed by the renewing of your mind." But that's because God's standard benefits you, not just her.

There are many practical, encouraging resources to help us in this area, including *Every Man's Battle* by Stephen Arterburn and Fred Stoeker. But I'm not going to spend the rest of this chapter talking about how we need to keep our thought lives pure, since most of us already know that. My main purpose is to help motivated, sensitive, and slightly clueless guys like you and me become more motivated, more sensitive, and slightly less clueless husbands by explaining the inner lives of the women we care about.

The hard truth is this: our wives and girlfriends *don't* just dismiss our sideways glances as a guy thing. Look at what one woman wrote us:

Beauty

I haven't been able to come to grips with my husband looking at other women. He is not into pornography, for which I am so thankful, but sometimes I see him looking for quite a bit longer than just a glance at other, younger women. I cannot describe the hurt I feel when he allows his eyes to take in every detail. I think otherwise very wonderful men don't stop to think about how this makes a woman feel. That figure my husband is looking at clarifies for me his deepest physical desires—and I look nothing like that. This leaves me feeling like I can never be what my loved one *really* wants.

It's News to Them...

I was also surprised at how many women had no idea that our visual wiring makes it difficult to not notice other women—and how many women have a really hard time with that knowledge. Remember, women *already* feel that they are in competition with every other beautiful woman—real or imagined—out there. Many women have told Shaunti and me that it's not that they walk around feeling violently suspicious of where we are looking as much as that they know they live in a culture saturated with options other than them. Shapelier options, racier options, younger options, easier options.

And now they know that the man they love is wired to notice every option. So when he does, it's hurtful.

> Women already feel that they are in competition with every other beautiful woman—real or imagined—out there.

When the Mirror Shatters

On our survey for this book, although two-thirds of women said they'd be bothered if their man noticed a woman with a great body, only one out of four said they'd be hurt. But when we asked how they'd feel *if they knew their man's thoughts were lingering on that woman's body,* the number of women who said they'd be hurt jumped to three out of four, with even higher rates among women under age forty-five. (Shaunti suspects that these numbers would be even higher if women could actually see inside our heads and watch our thoughts like a movie. I do too.)

Imagine [a situation where a woman with a great body walked into a room and your husband glanced several times at her.] Now imagine that you could magically see inside your husband/significant other's head. If you were to find out that his thoughts were lingering on that woman's body, would you find it hurtful? (Choose one answer.)

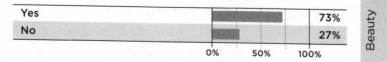

Yes	73%
No	27%

0%   50%   100%

Beauty

Truth is, most women can't comprehend why a man would choose or risk such damage. For many, lingering thoughts (and let's just admit it, lusting) were the same thing as cheating. "A woman whose husband doesn't control his looking and lusting will start to feel like a failure," one wife told us. "Why shouldn't she? Her beauty can no longer measure up to what her husband wants. His eyes speak volumes, so she has no choice but to doubt. But *she* wants to be found worthy in his eyes. *She* wants to be his beauty."

> "A woman whose husband doesn't control his looking and lusting will [feel she] can no longer measure up to what her husband wants."

As a man who, like you, wants to honor and show love to his wife, I find that woman's comment—and literally thousands more like it—very sobering. While most women don't mind if a husband or boyfriend is truly appreciating beauty (as in "What a beautiful girl!"), they experience pain if we look at, linger on, and lust after another attractive female. Their trust in their man's love gets badly shaken.

Shaking turns to breaking when the other woman or image obviously aims to *provoke* lust. That brings us to porn.

PORN SENDS HER A MESSAGE

"Let's face it," wrote one woman, "my husband can't control what woman will show up at what store or what street at a given time. It's not as though he's wishing that woman to appear. Porn, however, is different. Porn is a conscious choice. I think that when a man turns to porn, no matter how infrequently, it sends a clear message to his wife that she is inadequate. It says that no matter how she tries, she can't satisfy him sexually. Why should she bother trying?"

Unless a woman is naive about the power of porn or has become desensitized to it for other reasons, when her husband uses porn, it *feels* like cheating. And in truth, it *is* cheating. (Jesus's words come to mind here: "Anyone who looks at a woman lustfully has already committed adultery with her in his heart.") Even wives who don't equate pornography with adultery find the experience excruciating.

The fact is, for all men, this is an area where there has to be zero tolerance. Obviously that applies to pornography, but it also applies to lingering glances and lustful thoughts. We injure our wife when we look elsewhere for a thrill that we vowed to look for only in her. We break her trust. And we shatter our ability to reflect her beauty back to her.

Beauty

WE CAN SEND HER ANOTHER MESSAGE

Since our wife needs to know that we find her beautiful, and she feels protected by knowing that we only have eyes for her, well, we have plenty of opportunities these days to send her that message.

In the mid-1990s, *Sports Illustrated* did a cover feature entitled "The Trials of David" on David Robinson, the MVP center for the San Antonio Spurs. One segment of the article described how Robinson handled himself as a professing Christian, husband, and father in the midst of the NBA's intense temptations. For example, during television breaks, he would sit on the bench and stare at the floor in order to avoid looking at the gyrating cheerleaders on the court.

The article also mentioned that, like all NBA players, Robinson was constantly approached by attractive women who wanted to talk to him and were probably offering more than just witty conversation. Apparently he would rather brusquely brush them off. When asked to comment on that seemingly rude practice, he said, in effect, "If any woman is going to get her feelings hurt, *it's not going to be my wife.*"[7]

"If any woman is going to get her feelings hurt, *it's not going to be my wife.*"

A protector and hero in action.

Each day your wife and mine hold out to us their intense, God-given, little-girl desire (and right) to be treasured. Each day she's threatened on all sides by an offensive and abusive world. And each day—with kind words and faithful eyes—we, too, can be our wife's protector and hero.

9

THE MAN SHE HAD HOPED TO MARRY

What the woman who loves you most, most wants you to know

 n just a moment I'll share my biggest surprise from all my embedded-male research in interviews, surveys, and websites.

But before I do, I want to take you to a different data bank entirely: the mailbag of messages from wives and girlfriends who wrote and e-mailed Shaunti after reading *For Women Only*. Overwhelmingly, they relayed two things: how much they didn't know they didn't know and how much the relationship had changed once they understood their man's inner life—and started doing things differently.

THE CHANGE IN TWO
THAT STARTS WITH ONE

At various points in this book, you may have found yourself saying, "But if she would only be *reasonable,* I wouldn't have to do all this stuff you're telling me!" We sympathize with that sentiment, because Shaunti and I have each felt it at one time or another in our *own* learning process!

So many of the women who wrote to Shaunti described the same feeling: "This is unfair. Why do I have to do all the work?" But they also described how they came out the other side. Look at this excerpt from one e-mail:

> I fought my urge to defend myself and prayed that God
> would open my heart to consider the possibility that it was
> me, not my husband, who needed to change. And of course
> I immediately realized that was true. I was frustrated to
> know that I had behaved this way for five years of our
> marriage. But by the end of the book, I "owned" it. And I
> also realized that if I had the power to destroy my marriage,
> I now have the power to change and build it up again!

Guys, we could say the same thing. We don't have to wait until she completely understands us to see positive results. Now that we have more clarity about several key areas of her inner life and needs, the ball is in our court. We've now seen that you can be the only person to change in your relationship and *still* expect great new beginnings. Your marriage is definitely worth your taking the first step.[8]

Which leads me to the biggest surprise of all.

> The ball is in our court.

The One Most Important Thing...

As you can imagine, being an embedded male gave me lots of opportunities to be surprised. But nothing can compare to how I felt when I looked at the end of the survey. After two dozen multiple-choice questions, we gave the survey takers a blank space and asked, "What's the most important thing you wish your husband/significant other knew, but feel you haven't been able to explain in a way he understands?"

I assumed that the women would have plenty to say about what their husbands didn't understand, and in all honesty I had to gather my courage to look at the responses. And then I was astonished. Because the top thing that women wished their man knew was this:

▶ *You are my hero.*

Not always in those exact words, but invariably with that exact meaning. Over and over again, when women could say anything, they tried to express just how central their man was in their life, how much they admired, appreciated, and needed him, how much he made them happy, and how grateful they were for such a wonderful husband.

They were saying, in essence, that their husband really *is* the man they hoped he would be when they married him. Their average, ordinary guy—the person who sometimes leaves his fly down and the toilet seat up—*is* their knight in shining armor. Look at what this survey taker said she most wished her husband knew:

He has made me the happiest woman in the world.
I could have never asked for anything more. His love
and support throughout our marriage is more than any
woman could want. I am so lucky to have found him
thirty-two years ago.

◁ "He has made me the happiest woman in the world. I could have never asked for anything more."

There's no way in this short space to give you the same sense of awe I felt as I sat at my computer and scrolled through so many similar survey responses. Here are just a few examples:

- How deep my love and respect is for him.
- How much I appreciate him.
- How much I care for his happiness, feelings, and well-being.
- How happy he makes me.
- How much I respect him as a person.
- I would trust him with my life.
- My husband means more to me than words can say. He is the true essence of what I dreamed a husband would be when I was a little girl.
- I dearly appreciate his hard work.
- I feel incredibly lucky to be with him today.
- When he puts himself down, it hurts me—no one should say bad things about my favorite guy.

Conclusion

THEY FEEL IT BUT DON'T ALWAYS KNOW HOW TO SHOW IT

I had been skeptical when Shaunti proposed this idea, but she suspected from her talks at women's groups around the country that *most* women really do feel great respect and appreciation for their husband or boyfriend but don't always *show* it. Often women simply don't realize that some of their words or actions actually convey a lack of trust, when, as she says, "that is not the way they feel *at all*."

So on the survey we decided to ask the question directly and see what happened. Shaunti guessed that at least nine out of ten women would jump at the chance to confirm that they *did* respect and appreciate their husband or boyfriend.

And she was right.

Is this statement true or false? "Although I may not always show it well, I do deeply need, respect, and desire my husband/significant other." (Choose one answer.)*

True	93%
False	7%

* Excludes divorced/separated women (who still answered in the 80% range!).

0%   50%   100%

IN CLOSING...

I will leave you with this comment from one woman who spoke for many in trying to describe just how important her husband is to her:

My husband smiles at me when he comes home from work and discovers the kids have drawn monsters on my legs with markers. He appreciates egg sandwiches and

SpaghettiO's more than a gourmet meal. He believes that I am a better mother, more talented, and a more virtuous person than I actually am.... His eternal optimism changes me ever so slightly, day after day, into something much more beautiful than I'd otherwise be. He's imperfect, puerile, and sloppy, yet strong, wise, and loving.

The fact that I get to live with him over the course of my lifetime is one of the biggest scams I've pulled off—I keep waiting for him to wake up, jump over the mound of unwashed clothes, and bolt out the door. But he sees even my imperfections as endearing. Over the past ten years, we've both changed. But the one thing that remains constant is my utter and unashamed need of him.

Not to mention, he's really good in the sack.

Conclusion

Acknowledgments

Thousands of people provided the input and assistance that were crucial to the writing and content of this book, and there is no way to adequately thank all of them in this short space. To all of these wonderful folks, we want to say thank you, and we ask forgiveness in advance for the many we will not be able to name personally.

First, we must deeply thank and acknowledge our prayer team, who did the most important work by covering us in prayer during the original research and writing and for this revised edition. You have our deepest gratitude, and we, in turn, pray for great blessings on each of your lives.

The professional survey of women that is at the core of this book was guided by the experienced hand of Chuck Cowan of Analytic Focus (analyticfocus.com) and performed by Kevin Sharp and the rest of the team at Decision Analyst (decision analyst.com). As in all of our other books, I thank this excellent team.

We promised to keep the identity of the interviewees and focus group participants confidential, so we cannot name them here. Please know how much we appreciate all of you. We also are so appreciative of the many conference organizers, women's ministry directors, marriage pastors, and others who invited us to speak, allowing us to test, refine, and deepen our findings over the years.

Several individuals went above and beyond in providing assistance and help as we originally investigated the topics covered in this book. We need to especially acknowledge counselors Chris and Susan Silver of Tree of Life Ministries and Atlanta-based sex therapists and experts Dr. Douglas Rosenau and Dr. Michael Sytsma.

We are very grateful for the team that has come alongside to support and encourage us personally and professionally during the writing of both editions of this book, especially Shaunti's amazing staff team, led by her exceptional staff director, Linda Crews. Special thanks to Jenny Reynolds, whose help on deciphering brain science has been invaluable for so many of these books. We are also indebted to our special friends Eric and Lisa Rice, whose input, collaboration, encouragement, and friendship have been invaluable.

We are not quite sure how to adequately thank our exceptional editors, David and Heather Kopp, who went way, *way* above and beyond the call of duty, particularly the unexpected duty of taking a huge manuscript and turning it into a book that someone might actually be willing to read. To both of you: we are so grateful for your professional skills, your encouragement, and your friendship. Thanks to editors Amy McDonell, Eric Stanford, and Laura Wright for their hard work on this revision. We are also immensely grateful to the rest of the WaterBrook Multnomah family, especially Steve Cobb, Ken Petersen, Carie Freimuth, and Allison O'Hara, for their incredible friendship, support, and commitment to excellence. You all are such a pleasure to work with! Special thanks to Don Jacobson at the original Multnomah, whose leadership and friendship started this whole thing for us.

We also must express our incredible gratitude to our parents, to whom this book is dedicated: Bill and Roberta Feldhahn, and Richard and Judy Reidinger. You know we could never have written this book without each of you, who rode to the rescue time and again to help with kids, household chores, and editing input while deadlines loomed. We love each of you very much and are immensely grateful for your presence in our lives.

To our children, thank you for being such great kids and so understanding when Mom or Dad had to be locked away with a computer for hours at a time. We adore you and are so proud of the godly young woman and man you are and are becoming. We are so grateful to be on the adventure of life with you!

Finally, and most important, we lift up all praise and honor to the One who truly deserves it. If there is any eyeopening power in this book, it is because of the anointing of the Lord, who cares for His children and wants their relationships to be filled with joy.

Notes

1. *The Parent Trap,* directed by Nancy Meyers (Burbank, CA: Walt Disney Pictures, 1998).

2. The brain science in this chapter is simplified from an extensive review of research published in multiple journals, articles, and books. For example, the information on the effect of the ratio of gray matter to white matter in the corpus callosum comes from a study by University of Pennsylvania neuropsychiatrists: Ruben C. Gur et al., "Sex Differences in Brain Gray and White Matter in Healthy Young Adults: Correlations with Cognitive Performance," *Journal of Neuroscience* 19, no. 10 (May 15, 1999): 4065–72, www.jneurosci.org/content/19/10/4065. full.pdf. For more details on the different brain wiring of men and women in this area, written in laymen's terms, see the "Emotions" chapter of Shaunti's book *The Male Factor: The Unwritten Rules, Misperceptions, and Secret Beliefs of Men in the Workplace* (New York: Broadway, 2009).

3. See Douglas E. Rosenau, *A Celebration of Sex* (Nashville: Thomas Nelson, 2002). He addresses the physiological issues in more detail.

4. If you find yourself in the 25 percent of marriages where your wife is the one wanting more, and you would like a

resource that includes a discussion of that pattern, we recommend *A Celebration of Sex* by Douglas E. Rosenau.

5. Full quote: "The biochemical urge we call the sex drive comes in two basic styles: aggressive and receptive. The aggressive sex drive is controlled not just by testosterone, as most people think, but by vasopressin, DHEA, serotonin, dopamine, and LHRH as well. The receptive sex drive… has been overlooked altogether…. Receptive doesn't necessarily mean passive [but] available, and perhaps willing, but without the initiative to pursue sex" (Theresa L. Crenshaw, *The Alchemy of Love and Lust: Discovering Our Sex Hormones and How They Determine Who We Love, When We Love, and How Often We Love* [New York: Putnam, 1996], 125).

6. John M. Gottman and Nan Silver, *The Seven Principles for Making Marriage Work* (New York: Crown, 1999), 205–6.

7. The full quote reads, "I made a rule when I got married…. I decided that if anyone's feelings are going to be hurt, they're not going to be my wife's. If I think [a woman] is acting inappropriately, I say so. It may sound harsh, but that's the way it is. My wife is not going to be the one to suffer." David Robinson quoted in Leigh Montville, "The Trials of David," *Sports Illustrated,* April 29, 1996, 95.

8. For men who want to learn about certain areas in more detail, we list additional resources at formenonlybook.com. You may want to start with Emerson Eggerichs, *Love and Respect* (Brentwood, TN: Integrity, 2004), particularly the chapters written for men.

Dig deeper!

3 Video Studies with 6 Sessions Each

Shaunti Feldhahn

For Women Only

For Men Only and

For Couples Only

Video Study Pack

3-in-1 Relationship Study Resource with Companion DVD

Ideal for individuals or small groups, the *For Women Only, For Men Only and For Couples Only Video Study Pack* offers materials for women, for men, and for couples. This resource with DVDs and a participant's guide, fosters thoughtful inter-action, enabling couples to communicate better and embrace each other's differences.

Want her to REALLY understand you?

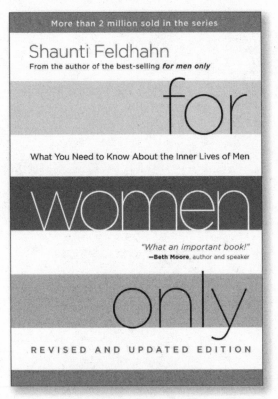

For Women Only offers fascinating insights into the hidden lives of men. Based upon a landmark nationwide poll, Shaunti Feldhahn provides groundbreaking information and advises how to convert her findings into practical application.

**Read an excerpt from this book and more at
www.WaterBrookMultnomah.com**

Also available from Shaunti!

Read excerpts from these books and more at
www.WaterBrookMultnomah.com

Shaunti Feldhahn Showed You How Men Think At Home —Now Find Out What They Think At Work

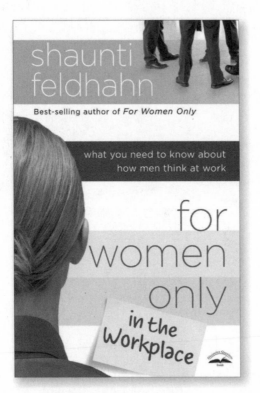

Do you know the unwritten rules of the workplace? *For Women Only in the Workplace* will equip you to be an effective Christian business-woman no matter what your circumstances.